ALA Editions • **SPECIAL REPORTS**

GRANT MONEY
THROUGH COLLABORATIVE
PARTNERSHIPS

NANCY KALIKOW MAXWELL

AMERICAN LIBRARY ASSOCIATION
Chicago   2012

In her thirty-year library career, **Nancy Kalikow Maxwell** has participated in successful grant projects totaling more than ten million dollars, with more than one million of those dollars flowing directly to the library. Formerly library director at Miami Dade College and Barry University, Maxwell currently owns and operates Kaliwell, Inc. (www.librarygrants.org), a grant development company that specializes in locating, writing, and evaluating grants for libraries and other educational organizations. A prolific writer, Maxwell has been published in the *National Catholic Reporter, Jewish Forward, Lilith, Moment,* and other periodicals. Her library publishing credits include the best seller *Sacred Stacks: The Higher Purpose of Libraries and Librarianship* (2006) and, as a contributor, *Writing and Publishing: The Librarian's Handbook* (2010) and *Librarians as Community Partners: An Outreach Handbook* (2010). A frequent contributor to *American Libraries* magazine, she has also authored two ALA Techsource *Library Technology Reports.* Maxwell can be reached at kaliwell@kaliwellinc.com.

Printed in the United States of America

16 15 14 13 12   5 4 3 2 1

Extensive effort has gone into ensuring the reliability of the information in this book; however, the publisher makes no warranty, express or implied, with respect to the material contained herein.

ISBNs: 978-0-8389-1159-4 (paper); 978-0-8389-9457-3 (PDF); 978-0-8389-9458-0 (ePUB); 978-0-8389-9459-7 (Kindle). For more information on digital formats, visit the ALA Store at alastore.ala.org and select eEditions.

Library of Congress Control Number: 2012010054

Series cover design by Casey Bayer.
Series text design in Palatino Linotype and Avenir by Karen Sheets de Gracia.

♾ This paper meets the requirements of ANSI/NISO Z39.48-1992 (Permanence of Paper).

To the memory
of my husband,
Rodney J. Maxwell,
1942–2009,
and to
Scott and Amanda,
who turned out great.
He would be proud.

CONTENTS

Acknowledgments   vii

1 **Introduction**   1

2 **Grant Development and Libraries**   7

3 **Finding Grant Developers for Collaboration**   17

4 **Working with Grant Developers**   29

5 **Research—The Librarian's Secret Weapon**   35

6 **Incorporating the Library into Grant Proposals**   43

7 **How the Library Can Support Grant Projects**   49

8 **Partnerships and Beyond**   55

9 **Grant-Writing Careers for Librarians**   63

10 **Conclusion**   69

Afterword   75

Selected Bibliography and Additional Sources   79

Index   83

ACKNOWLEDGMENTS

It was three years ago that acquisitions editor Stephanie Zvirin ran across my book *Sacred Stacks: The Higher Purpose of Libraries and Librarianship* at ALA Editions. "Has anyone contacted you about doing another project?" she asked. "If not, they certainly should have."

And for the next three years, she stayed with me, enduring all the twists and turns of my writing—or not writing—this book. First I said yes, then I said I couldn't, then I said I would, then I said I didn't know. Throughout, she persevered, staying with it through my various career obligations, retirement plans, and grant deadlines. And I'm glad she did. She is the best editor any writer could ever ask for. Thank you, Stephanie, for your persistence. It paid off.

I also thank Russell David Harper, my talented copy editor; he makes every sentence perfect—even this one.

I would also like to thank everyone at Barry University's Monsignor William Barry Memorial Library and Miami Dade College, especially at the North Campus and its library. Much of the knowledge I gained about grant development, administration, and evaluation came through opportunities provided at those institutions. For that, I am most appreciative.

A sincere thank-you to my colleagues in the grant-writing world, including those at the national level and in the Broward County chapter of the Grant Professionals Association.

To my many friends—thankfully too many to name—who made sure I was taken care of and well fed while I wrote this book, I am extremely appreciative.

To my family: daughter Amanda Maxwell and son Scott Maxwell (who give me *naches* and joy), mother Betty Kalikow, sister Barbara Kalikow Schwartz, brother Harvey Kalikow, cousin Judy Mesch, sister-in-law Elaine Miller—and all their spouses and children. You nurtured me throughout. I love you all.

INTRODUCTION

Groan. Not another book on library grants. Here you are struggling to run your library with 40 percent less than you received last year (and you are thankful you got that). The three-year hiring freeze has chilled your relationship with the staff to the point that even the ones who like you are grumbling. You want to retire, but the financial meltdown frizzled your funds to nothing. And now you are supposed to write grants. Fat chance, you say.

Save your disgruntlement for something more important—like getting a vanilla latte when you ordered chai tea. This book is not going to guilt-trip you over not bringing in grant money. And you won't be toiling over a tedious grant proposal, either. Instead, you will learn how to watch others do the toiling. Not that you'll be sitting back and doing nothing, but at least you'll benefit from the work of others who are writing grants. In this book, librarians will learn how to infiltrate the grant development process of other organizations and garner grant funds through them.

The idea for this book—like so much of life—came through happenstance. Though I am a highly successful grant writer—having helped bring in more than ten million dollars in grant funding for my library and college—my initial efforts at grant writing were failures. Lots of failures, if you must know.

But I persevered. After many grant-writing workshops and more disastrous grant attempts, I finally crafted my first successful proposal. The USDA—of all places—approved a grant for more than $150,000 to improve the science resources and services at my community college library.

My successful proposal not only garnered much-needed library materials but also elicited praise from the campus administrative dean. Personally, I was more interested in pleasing the dean than improving library resources, but it was nice to have accomplished both.

"You did an outstanding job with the USDA grant proposal," she wrote in an e-mail. "I was very impressed when I finished reading the entire proposal." Her compliment made my day, but what followed turned out to be of more lasting import.

"We are now working on a Title V grant," she explained. "A grant writing company has been hired to assist us. They have a lot of experience, but they will be requiring information from us periodically."[1]

They will be requiring information from us periodically.

That sentence changed the course of the library and my career. From those few words, I was able to participate in grant proposals netting more than ten million dollars to the college, with one million going directly to the library. Even better, I was able to write the book which you now hold in your hand (or view on your screen).

They will be requiring information from us periodically has become my maxim.

The need for information brought me to the grant table, where I was able to insert library funding into the grants under development. Being at the table made all the difference.

I am far from the first person to realize the importance of being where the action is, where money is discussed and divvied. The late visionary and library science professor Kathleen de la Peña McCook came to the same conclusion more than ten years ago. *A Place at the Table* she titled her plea, urging librarians to be present when decisions are made to build lasting communities.[2]

Years before McCook's book was published, two other librarian-authors—Patricia Senn Breivik and E. Burr Gibson—exhorted librarians to insinuate themselves into the process of garnering new funds from others.

"The library is uniquely suited to fare well in cooperative projects," they explained. "Library services and resources can be clearly shown in support of almost any aspect or program." However, the trick is to get the library included—either formally or informally—in the process. How reassuring, if not a little depressing, to find this suggestion in a 1979 ALA book entitled *Funding Alternatives for Libraries*.[3] Yes, we have been talking about finding other sources of revenue for decades.

LIBRARIES BRING IN MONEY

Libraries deserve to benefit financially from the work of others. As recent data shows, libraries contribute mightily to the economic value of those they serve. According to a study by the University of Pennsylvania, the Free Library of Philadelphia improved the economic value of the communities it served by more than $31 million.[4] Six million of those dollars resulted from workforce development activities, $3.8 million from business development activities, and the rest from improving reading and literacy skills.

The study also showed that, in Philadelphia, homes within a quarter mile of a library are worth $9,000 more than homes outside this range. Evidently, homeowners wanting to boost the value of their homes would be better off lobbying for a library branch in their neighborhood than upgrading their kitchen.

Though libraries are economic engines for their surrounding communities, they have yet to capitalize on their impact. The root problem, according to Steve Coffman, vice president at the library consulting firm LSSI (Library Systems and Services), is that the public library "is one of the few cultural or educational institutions to remain almost entirely dependent on local and state tax dollars." While museums, theaters, and zoos have diversified their revenue streams, libraries have yet to tap what he calls "plural funding," through gifts, fundraising, and foundations.[5]

Along with Coffman's suggestions, this book proposes another potential stream of funding for libraries to tap. By exploiting one of its greatest strengths—research ability—libraries can maneuver to the grant development table. For many librarians, conducting research is preferable to soliciting major gifts or forming a nonprofit to raise funds. Once at the table to present their results, they can divert some of the forthcoming funds to the library. The rest of this book provides instructions on how to go about accomplishing this.

HOW LIBRARIANS AND GRANT DEVELOPERS CAN HELP EACH OTHER: AN OVERVIEW

How Grant Developers Can Help Librarians

More Funding for the Library

Libraries can earn additional funds by being included in the grant development process of others. These funds could be used for library materials, equipment, staff, or programs. Or best of all, they could go directly into the library's general coffers for the library to use as it sees fit.

Of course, there is no guarantee a proposal will be successful. Even the most perfectly crafted applications are often turned down. As Stephen Seward, philanthropy director at the Nature Conservancy, notes, successful grant writing can seem like winning the lottery because it appears so illogical.[6]

It may look as if grants are awarded at random, but techniques and strategies exist to improve one's chances of success. Libraries can play a huge role increasing a grant's chances. As discussed below, libraries can help identify exactly the right grant opportunity for the applying institution. They can dramatically improve the proposal with solid research data. The librarian can keep the group on track and working within deadline. The library can create a new library activity or service, thereby improving the proposal along with the library. Once funds are appropriated, the library can help administer or evaluate portions of the project. Any of these avenues would improve the grant, potentially bringing in more funds to both the nonprofit organization and the library.

Strengthened Organizational Relationships

Even if the grant is not successful and no funds are awarded, the process of working with another organization to craft a grant proposal will enhance the relationship between the library staff and grant developer. Grant development usually includes intense, fevered work concentrated into a short span of time. Frequent meetings—via phone or e-mail, or face-to-face—are required to develop plans, share information, and review drafts. Assuming the library representative participating is congenial and effective (hopefully a correct assumption), the end result will be an enhanced relationship with the grant-seeking organization. Even if the initial venture is not successful, the next grant the organization embarks upon may include a library component, which could result in additional library funding.

Confidence to Develop Library Grants

When asked why they don't write grants, many librarians report the task is too daunting. The verb daunt (who knew that was a verb?) means "to drain the courage of, to intimidate or to dishearten"—an apt description of how many librarians feel when confronting a forty-page grant request-for-proposal due in three weeks. One book on the topic is called *Demystifying Grant Seeking,*[7] a title that suggests an unknowable, almost otherworldly pursuit.

After more than fifteen major grant initiatives, I still get a pit in my stomach when I review a new grant announcement. I can only imagine the aversion those not familiar with grant development must experience when contemplating the endeavor. Daunting, indeed.

But participating in someone else's grant provides an opportunity to learn the process without bearing the brunt of responsibility for the entire undertaking. Learning through observation—and participating on a more limited basis—allows neophytes to gain the confidence to undertake their own grant-writing projects in the future.

How Librarians Can Help Grant Developers

It is easy to see how new library funding, improved relationships, and grant-writing confidence benefit the library. What is less obvious is how the grant developer can benefit from the participation of the library. Though these benefits can be substantial, they usually go unrecognized. The burden, then, lies with the librarian to prove it. To use the business parlance of the day, libraries must convince others (and themselves) that they add value to the grant development process.

Research, Research, Research

All grants need some form of research to support the proposal. The ability of librarians to locate information will endear library professionals to grant developers forever. I do not use the word *endear* lightly. Many a reference librarian can recount an exuberant reaction to information they have produced.

Though it was years ago, I still remember one student's passionate response when I helped him locate information he was seeking. Standing over him at the computer, I suggested he try a combination of terms for his search. When he saw the citations that he needed appear, he bolted from his chair, grabbed my shoulders, and kissed me.

I have yet to be similarly embraced at any grant development meetings, but the presentation of data has often been met with the same kind of enthusiasm. When I distributed a copy of employment projections at one meeting, a faculty member kissed his fingers, saluted, and pronounced (in a fake foreign accent), "This is exactamemte what we need." Not exactly a smooch, but it felt good nonetheless.

Ready-Made Collaborative Partner

Libraries also bring to grant developers an organization to partner with. The trend in government granting and philanthropic giving is to require collaborative partners. To maximize effectiveness (known in plain English as getting more bang for the buck), many new funding sources require that more than one organization be included in and benefit from the project.

Making matters even worse for grant developers, announcements of grants requiring partners are often released with extremely tight deadlines. Because there isn't sufficient time to both find a partner and create a solid proposal, many grant developers simply pass on the possibility of applying for funding.

By simply being there as part of the process, the library could serve as the required partner. Much like those classic old movies where the beautiful young starlet comes into the room at exactly the right moment, libraries could have their moment in the spotlight just by being in the right place at the right time.

Source of Last-Minute Expenditures

Libraries could save the day by spending money!

To be deemed successful, grant-funded projects must not only attain the goals and objectives of the stated project but also spend all of the allocated funds within the granting period. One of the most egregious sins that a grant administrator can commit is to return unused funds to the granting agency. I have known more than one grant administrator who was terminated because large sums of grant funds went unexpended.

Libraries offer grant-funded projects an easy avenue to expend unused funds. Library materials can be purchased quickly and in varying amounts that would help out the grant project while also improving the library.

Stronger Relationship with the Library

Just as stronger relationships between collaborative partners benefit the library, so do they further the goals of the grant-developing organization. It is hard to imagine a nonprofit group, educational institution, hospital, or other organization that would not be improved through collaboration with a library. By availing themselves of library resources, services, publicity, and programming, such organizations will be able to fulfill their missions through closer interactions with the libraries that serve them.

Let's now look at the grant development process in more detail to see how organizations can work together and libraries can benefit from other people's money.

NOTES

1. Cristina Mateo, e-mail message to author, January 27, 2006.

2. Kathleen de la Peña McCook, *A Place at the Table: Participating in Community Building* (Chicago: American Library Association, 2000), 4.

3. Patricia Senn Breivik and E. Burr Gibson, "Operating within a Parent Institution," in *Funding Alternatives for Libraries,* ed. Breivik and Gibson (Chicago: American Library Association, 1979), 125.

4. Fels Research and Consulting, University of Pennsylvania, Fels Institute of Government, *The Economic Value of the Free Library in Philadelphia,* October 21, 2010.

5. Steve Coffman, as quoted in Irene E. McDermott, "Get Outta Here and Get Me Some Money, Too," *Searcher* 14, no. 7 (July/August 2006): 13–17.

6. Stephen Seward, as quoted in Judith B. Margolin and Gail T. Lubin, eds., *The Foundation Center's Guide to Winning Proposals II* (New York: Foundation Center, 2005), viii.

7. Larissa Golden Brown and Martin John Brown, *Demystifying Grant Seeking* (San Francisco: Jossey-Bass, 2001).

2

GRANT DEVELOPMENT
AND LIBRARIES

In order to benefit from other people's grants, you will need at least a rudimentary understanding of the grant development process. If you are a librarian, it is safe to assume that you will be able to locate sources about the grant development process for yourself, so what is provided here is simply an overview. As I mentioned earlier, however, the idea of writing a grant can overwhelm even the most seasoned professional. The abundance of books on the subject, though intended to calm fears, may have the opposite effect. Confronting a stack of publications on grant writing may dissuade you from even attempting such a project. But don't give up.

One of the best books on writing grants for libraries is *Winning Library Grants: A Game Plan.*[1] Some other good sources of information about grants are listed in the bibliography at the end of this book. Even better, try consulting a reference librarian (if you are not one yourself) for a list of sources. (Cautionary note: if you don't know a professional librarian who can provide such research, you may have difficulty benefiting from the advice provided in this book!)

For those who would rather not spend time reading about grants, this chapter provides a quickie summary of what you need to know to interject libraries into the process.

TYPES AND SIZES OF GRANTS

The word *grant* encompasses everything from a $100 donation to a multimillion-dollar federal construction project. One book on starting a grant-writing business lists sixteen categories of grants.[2] *Winning Library Grants* lists twenty typical categories.[3] Other sources categorize grants according to the type of giver, but even these categories can vary from publication to publication.

Among the most common major grant types by funding agency are

- government grants (federal, state, or local)
- corporate grants
- foundation grants
- private or individual grants

Some corporations and private individuals may give through foundations, which would make them foundation grants. Just to confuse matters, some municipal areas also support community foundations and provide funds locally, though these are not technically government grants. Fortunately for librarians looking for a collaborating partner, the category of the grant is not as important as other factors discussed here.

SIZE MATTERS

The amount of money given from a grant can vary widely. Most people assume a government or corporate grant will be substantial, but this is not always the case. It is true that many government agencies, such as the National Science Foundation or the U.S. Department of Education, offer grant programs in the millions of dollars, but they also administer programs that provide grants of just $1,000. Corporations, too, may be big in size but not big in giving. Many corporate gifts are less than $5,000. By the same token, while some private donors—also known as rich people—have been known to give huge amounts to institutions, others write checks for $50.

According to the Foundation Center, the median grant award is $25,000. The breakdown of these grants is as follows:

- 38%: $10,000–$24,999
- 23%: $25,000–$49,999
- 16%: $50,000–$99,999
- 17%: $100,000–$499,999
- less than 1%: more than $10 million[4]

From my own grant development experience—ranging from a request for $200 to a $4.5 million education grant—I can state emphatically that there is little correlation between amount of funds requested and the time required to develop the funding request. After spending two months preparing a grant for $168,000 and two months writing one for $1.2 million dollars, I realized that my grandmother was right. "It's just as easy to love a rich man as a poor one," she always said. Likewise, it is just as easy (or difficult) to write a grant for a lot of money as a little. Though I failed to take her up on the romantic advice, I urge you to take my grant-writing advice. If given the choice of working on a big grant or a small one, go for the big one. That is, unless the lesser grant comes with the possibility of spending time with an attractive potential suitor—in which case, see Grandma's advice.

GRANT DEVELOPMENT PHASES

The world of grant development is divided into three major phases: pre-award, grant development, and post-award.

1. Pre-Award

The *pre-award* phase includes all steps leading up to the actual grant development. Ideally, the institution will have in place a strategic plan and mission statement for the organization. These must serve as the foundation for any additional funding to be sought. Too often organizations experience what is called *mission creep,* where the group expands its mission to meet the requirements of the grant. To avoid this, only those grant sources that fit the goals and objectives of the organization should be pursued.

In addition to developing a strategic plan, other pre-award activities include

- identifying the need for the grant
- collecting data on the need for the grant
- locating the most appropriate sources of funding
- studying similar grant-funded projects
- analyzing the specific requirements of the grant under consideration
- aligning the organization's services with the potential grant
- conducting research on potential partners

The bridge that connects the pre-award phase to proposal development is the request for proposal, known in the grant world as the RFP. (Librarianship is not the only profession that loves acronyms.) The RFP is the bible of the grant development process. Because it lists all of the required components of the submitted document, it must be followed meticulously or, as grant expert Herbert B. Landau puts it, "religiously."[5]

2. Grant Development

Grant development is usually called *grant writing,* but the writing part is—or should be—the smallest component of grant development. Because grant development comprises several disparate elements, substantial time must be devoted to the development of the project. Though writing is one of the key elements, the other components demand more time. Unfortunately, more often than not, the looming deadline for submission prevents the grant developer from dedicating the amount of time needed. (More on this later.) But grants should not be written quickly. Rather, enough time should be allotted to perform the following steps:

- crafting the project to be funded
- identifying strategic partners
- identifying all individuals and departments involved
- planning for the project with all of the above
- compiling a meaningful budget
- establishing valid evaluation methods
- writing the grant
- submitting the grant

The final product of the grant process is not a technical monograph, position paper, or user's manual.[6] Rather, it should be a readable document written in plain English easily understood by nonexperts.

3. Post-Award

Post-award involves jumping, shouting, dancing, and opening and consuming of several celebratory bottles of champagne. High fives and congratulations from higher-ups usually follow. Once the hangover passes, the actual work on the grant begins. Usually included during this phase are

- publicizing the grant
- implementing the project
- receiving and spending grant funds
- evaluating the project
- reporting, reporting, and then reporting on the project
- sustaining the project

Ways the library can be involved in each of these steps are discussed in the following chapters. However, the majority of library involvement will most likely be during the other, earlier phases of grant development.

COMPONENTS OF GRANTS

Judith B. Margolin, vice president of the Foundation Center, calls the grant proposal a recipe. In order to be successful, she says, "all of the ingredients must be included. If something is left out, the final product won't come out quite right."[7] Though the terminology may differ, most grants call for the following major ingredients, which are described below along with examples from selected RFPs.[8]

Activities

The activities component of the grant proposal describes what will be done, by whom, and when. It is sometimes referred to as the plan of operation.

> *From criteria for a federal library grant—*
>
> Describe the project design. Provide a clear description of how the project objectives relate to the purpose of the program. Discuss the plan for managing the grant that ensures proper and efficient administration, including methods of coordination across organizational units.

Depending on the project and partners, the activities component may present an opportunity for library collaboration. Ideally, potential library activities will have been recognized before the grant team first meets. For instance, I was once asked to join a grant development group that was seeking funding to infuse science and technology into the preschool curriculum. Purchasing appropriate children's books and obtaining relevant science information for the teachers were two activities that had been identified for the library before the invitation was extended.

Unfortunately, most often the grant project under development does not include a clear-cut role for the library. In that case, it may be more difficult—but not impossible—to incorporate a library component into the project. Creativity from the library participants, and openness on the part of the grant developer, may lead to the inclusion of an appropriate library activity.

Budget

A grant's budget component is usually presented as both a numerical list and an explanation of how each amount was derived. It is a small portion of the complete package, but it can take a huge portion of the time to prepare.

> ### From criteria for a federal U.S. Homeland Security grant—
>
> Funds can be used only for procurement of equipment. No funds can be used for labor, overhead, travel, or other expenses. Include separate columns for each source of funding, i.e. industry partners, other matching funds.
>
> ### From criteria for a National Science Foundation grant—
>
> Funds will not be provided for equipment purchases. Significant faculty involvement is essential . . . and should be reflected in the budget requested.

Narrative

The body of the proposal is the narrative. Just as a good novel keeps the reader's interest, the narrative section of the grant should be easily understood and of interest to the readers. Because grants are often reviewed by nonexperts, the narrative (not to mention the entire proposal) should be written using lay language.

Several sections make up the narrative, which can include the needs statement, activities, personnel, publicity, sustainability, and outcomes and evaluation. (Each of these elements is discussed separately in this section along with examples.) However, not all proposals include all of these elements within the narrative. Some proposals call the project activities the narrative. Others may pull out the needs statement, publicity, or evaluation components as stand-alone elements. Since such variety exists, careful attention should be paid to the specific requirements of each RFP.

Needs Statement

The needs statement is the element of a grant that absolutely cries out for librarian assistance. Like other librarians, I cringe when others conduct so-called research by typing a string of words into Google. Many RFPs require solid data to substantiate need. The request will be strengthened and chances for success improved by the inclusion of specific research findings identified by a professional librarian. This type of information cannot usually be found through a simple Google search and instead must be located using a library's subscription databases or other specialized resources that nonlibrarians cannot easily access.

From the library perspective, the more information a needs section requires the better. Some grant announcements require only a broad description of the need for the project. But other grants will enumerate precisely what types of data are required—which is where the expertise of the librarian comes in.

> ### From criteria for a state grant application—
>
> To give a clear picture or description of the need, provide who is the target population that the project is intended to reach. Include information on the size of the population, characteristics, statistics or other demographics of the group to be served. What are the unmet needs of the target population, including information on education levels, access to resources, community situation, education, etc.?

Personnel

The category *personnel* includes all individuals to be involved in the proposed project, including those who will be paid from grant funds and others who will donate their time (in what are known as in-kind contributions). Resumes or biographical paragraphs describe their qualifications.

> ### From criteria for a federal education grant—
>
> "Quality of personnel" should include:
>
> 1. Qualifications required of the project director, including formal training or work experience in fields related to the objectives of the project . . .
> 2. Qualifications required of each of the other personnel to be used in the project . . .
> 3. Plan for employing personnel who have succeeded in overcoming barriers similar to those confronting the project's target population.

Publicity

The publicity component explains how others will learn about the project.

> ### From criteria for a state library grant—
>
> Describe plans to promote and publicize the project. . . . Tell how the target audience will be informed about the project.

Outcomes and Evaluation

The outcomes and evaluation component explains how the funders and others will know if the project has been successful.

> ### From criteria for a National Science Foundation grant—
>
> Provide an evaluation plan that will inform the project progress and measure its impact. Include a description of the instruments/metrics used to measure, document, and report on the project's progress.

Even this component might present an opportunity for library-based research. For instance, one grant to encourage women to pursue science careers required that the outcomes be related to the "present state of science education" and "contribute to the development of effective techniques and approaches to science education." Research conducted by librarians on the status of current science education and effective techniques would strengthen this section of the grant proposal.

Summary

The summary describes, in one paragraph or one page, the central focus and activities of the project. One seasoned grant professional I know says that if you can't explain your grant in one or two sentences, the grant needs more work. And because several people in the grant-reviewing process will rely on the summary statement, it must be not only succinct but comprehensive. In fact, an incorrectly executed summary can have dire consequences.

> *From criteria for a National Science Foundation grant—*
>
> The project summary must specifically discuss in a separate labeled section the intellectual merit and broader impacts of the proposed activities. Proposals that fail to do so will be returned without review.
>
> *From criteria for a state library grant—*
>
> Provide a concise summary of the project in a few sentences. Indicate what you plan to do, and who will benefit.

Sustainability

The sustainability component outlines how the project will be continued beyond the grant-funded period.

> *From criteria for a state library grant—*
>
> Describe plans to continue the project once grant funding ends.

LIBRARIES AND THE GRANT PROCESS

Helping Grant Developers

Grant professionals often specialize in one phase of the grant development process. Some may excel at developing the proposal but lack the ability to locate the best source in the pre-award stage. Others may possess expertise in administering grant-funded projects—which often requires an understanding of complicated accounting and reporting procedures—but lack skills in grant identification. Most grant professionals concentrate on the proposal development phase, but they may also be called upon to perform functions during the pre-award or post-award stage, or both.

No matter which phase they work in, few grant professionals are masters of all. Even if they have experience with all phases, few have the time to do all of them. This is where librarians come in. Librarians could assist by interjecting themselves into the grant process in the areas the professional lacks, thereby benefiting both the process and—hopefully—the library.

Libraries and the Pre-Award Phase
Libraries can gain their entrée into the process through their unique ability to locate funding sources. "I'm looking for a grant," coming from a grant seeker, should be heard as magic words for librarians, possibly beginning a dialogue between the seeker and librarian that could lead to grant collaboration.

Some other pre-award activities that could benefit from library involvement include studying similar grant-funded projects, documenting the need for the project, and conducting research on potential partners—all of which are described in more detail later.

Libraries and the Proposal Development Phase
To be involved in the next phase—proposal development—a library representative needs to be at the table. As a partner in the process, the librarian will be in a position to insert the library into the proposal under development. Finessing one's way into someone else's grant process requires diplomacy, courage, and guts. When it comes to getting the library included, no substitute exists for being involved physically—or at least virtually via phone or computer—where the action is.

Once at the table, the librarian is in a position to help. Any phase of the proposal development listed above can provide opportunities. Depending on the skills and talents of the person at the table, this participation could range from finding a place for the grant team to meet to recording minutes. Budget preparation is a particularly crafty assignment for the librarian to accept because it affords an opportunity to insert line items for library materials, programs, and services.

Libraries and the Post-Award Phase
Libraries can also participate in other people's grants during the post-award phase by helping to publicize or evaluate the project. Bear in mind, however, that this involvement would need to be spelled out in the original grant proposal. Additional possibilities for library participation in the post-award phase are discussed in chapter 7.

NOTES

1. Herbert B. Landau, *Winning Library Grants: A Game Plan* (Chicago: American Library Association, 2011).
2. Preethi Burkholder, *Start Your Own Grant-Writing Business* (New York: Entrepreneur Press, 2008), 17–18.
3. Landau, 6–7.

4. As quoted in Burkholder, 58.

5. Landau, 50.

6. Robert S. Frey, *Successful Proposal Strategies for Small Businesses,* 4th ed. (Boston: Artech House, 2004), 339.

7. Judith B. Margolin and Gail T. Lubin, eds., *The Foundation Center's Guide to Winning Proposals II* (New York: Foundation Center, 2005), xii.

8. The examples are taken from CISE Pathways to Revitalized Undergraduate Computer Education, National Science Foundation, April 22 , 2010; Emergency Communication and Alert Equipment for State University System of Florida and Florida Community College Campuses, U.S. Department of Homeland Security, April 3, 2006; LSTA Guidelines, Florida Secretary of State, April 21, 2010; Minority Science and Engineering Improvement Program, U.S. Department of Education, April 24, 2008; Upward Bound Program, U.S. Department of Education, January 27, 2011.

3

FINDING GRANT DEVELOPERS

FOR COLLABORATION

Now that you are convinced that you want to collaborate with another organization on its grants, you need to know where to find one. Potential grant partners can be found in libraries and beyond. Let's start with the ones within the library walls.

GRANT DEVELOPERS IN LIBRARIES

The best place to find an organization crafting a grant proposal is in the library. Not any library, of course. And not all libraries are harboring grant-writing organizations. But grant developers can be found in a few specialized libraries, beginning with the Foundation Center's network of funding information centers.

Foundation Center Cooperating Collections

Founded in 1956, the Foundation Center is a leading source of information about philanthropy worldwide. Supported by more than five hundred different foundations, the center maintains databases on foundations and donors, teaches courses on grant-related topics, and conducts research on foundations and the nonprofit sector.

For grant-developer-seeking purposes, the most important activity of the Foundation Center is its operation of Library/Learning Centers and Cooperating Collections. Like bees to honey, grant developers are drawn to these locations because of their enticing grant resources. Especially sweet are the resources offered at each of the five Library/Learning Centers. Those lucky enough to be near the metropolitan areas of New York City, Washington DC, Atlanta, Cleveland, and San Francisco will find free access to an extensive array of Foundation Center resources and educational programs.

For those outside these metropolitan areas, the Foundation Center operates a network of more than four hundred Cooperating Collections spread out across the country—and the world. Located in public libraries, community foundations, and educational institutions, this network of information centers provides free access to print and online resources. A complete listing of Cooperating Collection locations can be found at the center's website.[1] The Foundation Center is always looking for additional locations, so libraries that meet the criteria found at its site may want to consider joining the network.

All Foundation Center Cooperating Collection locations offer what is called a *core collection*. The core collection includes several thousand dollars' worth of online and print resources that are invaluable for those seeking a grant. At each Cooperating Collection location, nonprofit organizations are provided free access to two Foundation Center databases, the Foundation Directory Online and Foundation Grants to Individuals Online. Foundation Directory Online contains comprehensive information on more than 100,000 foundations and donors, including details on more than two million grants.

Foundation Grants to Individuals Online provides students, artists, and researchers with information on more than 7,500 funders and opportunities. When I participate in training sessions on these two databases, I find interest in this latter resource intense. Participants politely follow along as the grants directory is explained. But when the product for individuals is unveiled, everyone perks up and questions begin flying.

"Does this have scholarships my daughter could apply for?"

"Are there travel grants to Italy in here?"

"Can I get money to pay for my electricity?"

When they hear the answers yes, yes, and maybe, the interest level goes from polite to enthusiastic.

Because of the extensive information provided at Foundation Center locations, nonprofit organizations visit them often, making them perfect places to connect with a grant collaborator. Think of them as the equivalent of a singles bar. Librarians looking to "hook up" with a nonprofit organization should consider seeking out these locations.

"What's your astrological sign?" may not be the best opening line to use. But "Do you come here often?" may work just fine. Remember that anyone consulting a Foundation Center Cooperating Collection has come there seeking information on some aspect of grant or nonprofit development. Since you are seeking someone seeking this information, no better place can be found to locate a potential grant collaborator.

Reference Desk

Your own library's reference desk may be the next best place to find a grant developer. Perhaps at this very moment, one of the reference librarians is at the desk helping a faculty member find a sabbatical travel grant to France (with the first reference interview question being, "Can I come, too?"). Or maybe you are the reference librarian who just last week helped the new American Red Cross director find a grant source for an emergency awareness campaign.

Public libraries are often the first place grant seekers consult to find information on a grant. They may be looking for a source of funding or data to support a grant application. But public libraries are not the only types of libraries that assist with grant development. Academic libraries, special libraries, and school media centers are also sought out by those looking to find or support a grant-funded project.

At the community college where I worked, academic department chairs and faculty were encouraged (to put it lightly) to seek grant funding for new projects. To begin this task, they often turned to the library to help them find an appropriate source.

Medical libraries can be good sources of information on research funding, and they are excellent resources for those preparing literature reviews to support research proposals. Teachers may seek out the school media center to find potential sources of funding. Especially needed these days are sources of support for supplies that, in the wake of budget cuts, are no longer provided.

Capturing Reference Desk Information on Grant Seekers

Though potential grant partners may be as close as your own reference desk, a disconnect often keeps this information from reaching the appropriate person in the library. I recently conducted a workshop on library grant collaboration where several reference librarians and circulation technicians mentioned this problem. Though they may have information about individuals within their organizations working on grants, they did not feel a need to pass on such information. Nor had any of them been asked by a library administrator if any grant seekers had visited the library.

To capitalize on this potential source of information, a system needs to be put in place to forward details about grants under development that become known by the frontline library staff. A formal system, such as a written form or contact log, could be maintained with information about the grant seeker. Or the "system" might consist of periodic calls to the public service points, asking, "Have you helped someone working on a grant?" Whichever type of information-gathering technique is chosen, the end result should be intelligence about grants being sought or developed.

GRANT DEVELOPERS BEYOND THE LIBRARY

Once you have exhausted the library as a source of grant developers, you will need to venture out beyond the library walls. Searching for a potential partner outside of the confines of the library can be done by locating a grant writer, locating an organization that has previously submitted a grant, or finding an organization developing a grant.

Finding a Grant Writer

When Alexis de Tocqueville visited America in the 1830s, he admired the spirit of voluntary association exhibited among Americans. The veracity of his observation continues to this day. In the world of grant writers, as in many other professions, voluntary associations abound.

Grant Professionals Association

Several professional organizations serve those developing, writing, managing, or evaluating grants and contracts. One of the most prominent of these associations is the Grant Professionals Association (GPA; the former Association of American Grant Professionals). In addition to the national office, GPA is structured by local chapters operating within metropolitan areas or counties. A local chapter would be one of the best places to find a potential grant collaborator. Listings of these chapters can be found at the GPA website.[2]

Once a local group is identified, librarians can choose from a variety of strategies to approach them. The first—and easiest—way is to simply join the organization. In recognition of the synergy between librarians and grant professionals, GPA recently announced a reduced membership fee for members of the American Library Association. By joining GPA, attending meetings, and participating in programs and events, librarians will gain easy access to information about local grants under development.

American Grant Writers' Association

The American Grant Writers' Association (AGWA) is another membership association for grant professionals. Specializing in those who research grants and write proposals, AGWA is not structured through chapters. However, information about the group's state networking chairpersons and fields of interest networking chairpersons can be found at the AGWA website.[3]

Association of Fundraising Professionals

The Association of Fundraising Professionals (AFP) represents 30,000 members working in all aspects of philanthropy. For a list of the group's more than 200 chapters, visit the AFP website.[4] AFP is not exclusively focused on grant development but rather addresses all aspects of raising funds. However, grant writers are included in the membership, so librarians seeking grant professionals could reach out to this group.

Finding an Organization That Submitted a Grant

Because grant development is so complex, some organizations never get involved in grants. Others do it all the time. To find a grant-in-development, it would behoove you to find an organization that has experience developing and submitting proposals. The grant professionals groups listed above will yield information on organizations that fit that description.

Other sources for information on grants-in-development include previous grant award winners, grant program officers, grant evaluators, and grant reviewers.

Previous Grant Award Winners

Most funders provide information about award winners to publicize their grant program and highlight innovative projects they have supported. Check the website of a government agency or grant-giving foundation that has supported projects in your area. Once you have located information about their grants, click on the previous awards section.

Grant Program Officers

Wise grant developers will check with the funding agency before launching into a grant project to see if it meshes with the agency parameters. The agency's program officers may know of individuals who in previous granting cycles have been awarded grants in your area. You must keep in mind, however, that in most grant-funding competitions it is absolutely, positively illegal for those receiving or reviewing grants to reveal anything about the proposals submitted. Likewise, it is ill advised for anyone developing a grant to discuss the project with anyone who does not absolutely need to know. Confidentiality must be maintained throughout the process by both the grant developer and the granting agency. Ethical funding agency personnel would never reveal who has applied for funding, the amounts requested, or any details about a proposed project. By the same token, grant developers should never ask a funding agency what other agencies have applied or for information about possible competitors. However, inquiries about previous grant winners—information that is publicly available—is fair game.

Grant Evaluators

Major grant-funded projects are often evaluated by an entity outside of the organization. Also known as external evaluators, these individuals act much like a financial auditor and strive to determine if the project is programmatically and fiscally on track. Because their livelihoods depend on grants, evaluators should be in the know about grants previously awarded. To find a grant evaluator in your area, you can consult the American Evaluation Association or try one of the associations for grant writers discussed above.[5] When you contact them, remember to restrict any inquiries to former grants rather than those currently in development.

Grant Reviewers

Most government granting agencies use grant reviewers to help decide who gets funded. As mentioned above, because the information about proposals that have been reviewed is confidential, grant reviewers will not be able to provide any specific details about who submitted grant proposals or the content of the grant. However, those who have reviewed grants may be able to discuss in general the types of agencies that tend to submit grants. Carefully parsed, this information may provide leads to grant-developing organizations.

Finding an Organization Developing a Grant

Librarians can find potential collaborative grant developers through the nonprofit universe. Vast and varied, the world of nongovernmental organizations (or NGOs) can be difficult to negotiate. Because of the size and structure—or rather lack thereof—of the nonprofit sector, finding a local group can be frustrating. Also difficult may be posing the question about grants-in-development, because many organizations try to keep this information under wraps, lest someone else steal their idea. Asking broadly about grants in general will be less threatening than asking about specific projects under development.

One of the best places to begin your search is with a local nonprofit organization clearinghouse, which itself is usually a nonprofit organization. The United Way is often the major clearinghouse of organizations in a community, but there may be others in your area. Don't forget that standard reference source, the *Encyclopedia of Associations*. What you need to find is a nonprofit organization of nonprofit organizations. (That is not an erroneous duplication of words—there are nonprofits of nonprofits.)

Information and Referral Clearinghouses for Nonprofit Organizations

In many communities, one information and referral organization will provide comprehensive information about local organizations. Because they often serve as emergency switchboards, they maintain information about all of the major service providers in an area. You will be able to locate a local clearinghouse through the Alliance of Information and Referral Systems (AIRS). To find participating information and referral organizations, consult the AIRS online member directory.[6]

Many of these groups also participate in the 2-1-1 telephone referral system.[7]

Other Sources of Information on Nonprofit Organizations

In many local areas, coalitions have been formed that operate much like formal clearinghouses. These can take the form of subject-specific coalitions (such as human services coalitions), type-of-activity coalitions (such as chambers of commerce), or geographic coalitions (such as tourism bureaus).

Because there are so many of these types of groups, examples of organizations to approach are provided here. Listed in alphabetical order, these are intended as starting places only. As you review this list, try to think of groups or cooperative agencies in your own area that could be sources for grant developers. With a little creativity and innovative thinking, you may be able to picture additional possibilities.

ADVISORY COMMITTEES
Large-scale projects and cross-agency initiatives frequently solicit opinions from advisory committees. Since representation on these bodies comes from community organizations, advisory committees may yield ideas for potential grant-developing groups.

BOARDS/GOVERNING AGENCIES
Grant-giving organizations are often governed by boards made up of organizational representatives or individuals. State and local agencies may also report to a board of directors. Individuals involved in these groups are obviously involved in their community, so they may be able to provide leads about others who are developing grants.

CIVIC ASSOCIATIONS, NEIGHBORHOOD COUNCILS, EMPOWERMENT ZONES
These gatherings of citizens in a limited geographic area are dedicated to improving the quality of life for those within their borders. Because neighborhood improvement often involves grant-funded projects, contacting these groups may prove fruitful.

LEGISLATIVE HEARING TESTIFIERS
Grants often begin with the recognition of a social problem. In a democracy, one potential avenue for fixing the problem is through legislation proposed on a local, state, or federal level. Once these solution-posing bills are proposed, everyone has a chance to express an opinion through legislative hearings. Nonprofit organizations invested in solving the problem often testify at these hearings. These same types of groups often seek funding to address the problem through grants. Therefore, legislative hearings present opportunities to find potential grant seekers. To find such groups, search the public record for organizations that provided hearing testimony on a bill of interest.

LEGISLATORS
Many institutions routinely seek out endorsements from elected officials prior to submitting a grant proposal. Therefore, legislative offices are good places to check for grant

leads. Once again, asking for specific information about the submitting agency or project topic is verboten. However, you are free ask for the names of the key players in the legislator's district.

LOCAL, TOWN, AND COUNTY OFFICIALS

Especially in these tight economic times, many government agencies need to supplement their support through grant funding. Larger communities may employ a grants department, while others may assign this duty to individuals in other departments. Task forces, citizen boards, and subject-specific committees, such as transportation or elderly services, may also be sources to check.

NONPROFIT ROUND TABLES

Many communities maintain forums for nonprofit agencies to meet and discuss topics of common concern. These round tables, which are similar to the information and referral clearinghouses discussed earlier, can be invaluable for finding grant developers. The trick is finding them. Because they are often informal gatherings known of only by attendees, they can be difficult to uncover.

PARENT-TEACHER ASSOCIATIONS

Always short of cash, parent-teacher associations are ripe for grant funding. Many pursue funding alternatives to support student needs.

UNITED WAY

As the major umbrella organization for nonprofits, the United Way is a good place to begin a search for grant developers in any community.

VENDORS

In previous library jobs, the local book sales representative was my main source of gossip about other libraries in the area. The same can be true for information about grants-in-development. Because grants are used to purchase things, vendors may have knowledge of past projects. It never hurts to ask. If nothing else, you may get some juicy gossip about the library down the street.

Finding a Project That Needs a Partner

If you have not been successful finding a potential grant developer through any of the avenues above, the final option is to find a project in need of a grant, which could then form the basis for a grant partnership with the library.

Meet a Library Need

The best way to find a potential project partner (pardon the "p's") is to first figure out the most pressing need in the library. For instance, at my college library, students who were parents would often bring their children with them to the library. While the parents tried to study, the children would quickly grow bored, becoming noisy and disruptive. What was needed was a collection of children's books, which could be used to distract them, if only for a little while, while their parents and others in the library studied.

Rather than writing a grant solely for children's resources in the library, other departments of the college that would benefit from a children's collection were identified. The on-campus preschool and early childhood education departments came to mind. Using several of the tactics discussed in this book, these departments were approached. The result was a million-dollar proposal for various educational services, including a children's book collection. Unfortunately, the grant was not funded, but the proposal led to other successful collaborations between the library and those departments.

Address a Public Policy Issue

Another source of ideas for grant-funded collaborative projects is the political process. Grants are not given in a vacuum. Rather, in our country grants are conceived of and administered by the government or other funding agency in response to a perceived need. This realization was underscored for me when a grant writer I know moved to France and could not find a job in her new country. "They don't give grants here the way we do," she reported.

In America, social problems on the public's mind or in the media are often accompanied by funding. For instance, two major social issues have been in the news recently: childhood obesity and the need for more STEM (science, technology, engineering, and mathematics) education. Substantial amounts of funding are available to solve both problems.

The library could benefit from this reality by identifying a pressing social problem and devising a solution that involves the library. For instance, childhood obesity could be tackled through parent education, nutrition demonstrations, or book collections at fitness centers. A myriad of STEM programs, including space for tutoring, homework help, or new science resources, could be instituted. Once the library portion is conceived, the next step to creating a collaborative project is to identify the other major players in the community.

MANEUVERING TO THE TABLE

Subtlety Needed

Once you have located an individual or organization, the next question is how to approach them. "Hey, baby. Want to collaborate?" is not exactly appropriate, but it is the essence of what you are trying to communicate.

To get there, a gentler, subtler approach is called for. *The Librarian's Guerrilla Guide to Grants* was a working title for this publication at one point, in recognition of the infiltration aspect being called for here. Other images that convey the approach needed are a wolf in sheep's clothing or a Trojan horse. Once allowed in the door, the librarian is ready to spring loose. But first you need to get inside. Whichever metaphor is used, finesse and cleverness are required elements. Just make sure your finagling is done with a positive attitude. Yes, you are trying to get something for the library. But the library, too, has a lot to offer. As Marylaine Block reminds us in *The Thriving Library*, "Libraries in fact are attractive partners."[8]

What Can the Library Do for You?

Millions of dollars of market research preceded the United Parcel Service ad campaign slogan "What can Brown do for you?" Libraries can save all that money by keeping that same motto in mind when approaching potential grant partners. Too often librarians underestimate the value they bring to projects and services. Don't forget that libraries are "uniquely suited" for cooperative efforts and that, in fact, library services and resources can support almost any aspect of a program.[9]

Before you approach a grant-developing organization or individual, try to figure out what the library can do for this potential partner. If you cannot think of a clear role that can be expressed in just a few words, keep looking until you find an angle. Here are some possibilities to consider.

Library Research

As I will detail in chapter 5, the ability of libraries to conduct research and present findings relevant to grant identification and preparation is pivotal. See that chapter for details on how best to deploy this strategy.

Writing and Editing Assistance

As anyone who has served on a reference desk can testify, library users assume librarians are good editors and proofreaders. More times than I can count, I have been asked to look over someone's sentence, paragraph, or entire paper. Because my college served many non–English speakers, grammar assistance was frequently sought at the desk. Librarians are also asked for assistance because the public perception is that those in the profession are intelligent and articulate (would that it were uniformly true!). Capitalizing on this reputation, librarians could approach grant developers with an offer to look over the developing grant for editing or to catch grammatical errors.

Bring Parties Together

Libraries are uniquely positioned as neutral territory within communities. Because most community organizations view the library positively and as nonthreatening, libraries can easily become a central gathering place for competing community organizations. Positioning itself as a "Switzerland of the nonprofit world," the library could capitalize on its perceived neutrality by providing a place for groups to gather.

Therese Purcell Nielsen at the Huntington Public Library (New York) did exactly that. As a Foundation Center Cooperating Collection, the library encouraged nonprofit groups to gather on its premises. By providing a forum for organizations to discuss common problems and concerns, Nielsen positioned the library as the focal point among different groups.[10]

Become a Matchmaker

Going one step beyond simply providing a place for gathering, the library could actually bring together partners. Again, through its unique provision of service to all, the library may know about the projects and programs of a variety of organizations. As long as the library does not breach privacy or confidentiality, it may be in a position to forward information about one organization to another group. Of course, permission would need to be secured before any information could be revealed. Once given the go-ahead, the library could become the catalyst for productive partnerships, with both parties beholden to the library for bringing them together.

By way of an example, let's say a new staff member of the local Lung Association comes to your library. Hoping to launch an extensive outreach service, she needs to know how much a new van would cost. The next week the election commission calls to schedule a visit of the "voter motor" mobile registration van at the library.

In the matchmaking role, you could suggest that the voter van could also distribute information about the Lung Association. Or maybe the Lung Association could encourage voter registration. After obtaining permission from both groups, the library could provide the respective contact information so further discussions could ensue. Perhaps nothing concrete will come of it, but it is worth a try. Going one step further, if a project develops, the van could even be stocked with library books on health and voting.

Another example would be if a college's drama department wanted to find a grant to create an endowed chair. One of the first steps would be to list the types of organizations that would benefit from such a venture, such as local theaters, arts patrons, and actors' associations. Or if a community organization wanted to begin a gardening project, the library could find local farm organizations, gardening clubs, and youth services agencies (which could provide for free labor). These groups can then be brought together, with the library as the middleman.

The library can help identify these groups only if it is aware of the need. This type of information could be obtained through informal conversation—"So, what are you working on in your department?" Or it could be obtained through a more structured approach. College libraries could send periodic surveys to the school's academic departments soliciting information about any partner agency needs. Or the question could be posed at an academic managers' meeting. No matter how the information is obtained, the library needs to be aware of these needs before it can hope to benefit from any potential collaborations.

NOTES

1. For a complete list of cooperating collections, go to http://foundationcenter.org/collections/.

2. GPA chapter listings may be found at http://grantprofessionals.org/membership/chapters-membership-tab.

3. See http://www.agwa.us/aboutus.

4. See http://www.afpnet.org/audiences/chapters.cfm.

5. For the American Evaluation Association, see http://www.eval.org/.

6. See the "I&R Directory" at http://www.airs.org/.

7. See http://www.211.org/.

8. Marylaine Block, *The Thriving Library: Successful Strategies for Challenging Times* (Medford, NJ: Information Today, 2007), 105.

9. Patricia Senn Breivik and E. Burr Gibson, "Operating within a Parent Institution," in *Funding Alternatives for Libraries,* ed. Breivik and Gibson (Chicago: American Library Association, 1979), 125.

10. As posted on Foundation Center CC Talk Message Board, July 14, 2010.

4

WORKING
WITH GRANT DEVELOPERS

I f you have successfully followed the steps outlined in this book so far, you should be ready to collaborate on a grant. Grant development efforts are usually undertaken by teams or by individual grant developers, both of which you will need to know about. Suggestions on working with both types are provided below.

GRANT DEVELOPMENT TEAMS

Collaborative grant teams "sometimes feel like a ten-car pileup," admit grant developers Karen Stinson and Phyl Renninger.[1] Especially when the grant proposal is not coming together—which unfortunately happens often—the group approach can appear unproductive and inefficient. Nonetheless, grant development by teams is still the recommended method.

"A group working collectively is smarter than any person or group who works individually," Stinson and Renninger remind us. "A design team can provide diversity of ideas and opinions and provide unique solutions because there are many different views that can be presented by the people in the team."[2]

Though there is no formal name for groups that develop grants, the terms *project teams, grant development groups,* and *design teams* are common. Whatever they are called, these gatherings include individuals representing various organizations, possessing specific knowledge or talents, or having a stake in the project under development.

Grant teams are usually directed by the person with overall responsibility for putting the grant together, be that a professional grant writer or project coordinator. Unfortunately, I have suffered through several grant development teams with no designated leader. Most often someone in the group will have located a grant opportunity and called the group together, but the e-mail announcing the meeting will include the caveat "I can't chair this, but let's get together and talk about it." Or, worse, the meeting will open with such a disclaimer.

In these leaderless groups, an informal chairperson sometimes emerges from those assembled. However, if no one claims the leadership role, the group can dissolve on its own accord. This vacuum provides an excellent opportunity for the library representative, should he or she be so predisposed to lead the effort. More on claiming other roles within the group is discussed below.

Just as there is no standard name for these groups, there are no formal membership criteria. Most often the key individuals in grant teams will be

- content experts
- budget and finance experts
- grant development experts
- grant administrators, or those knowledgeable about the funding source
- partner agencies
- service recipients
- editors, writers, proofreaders[3]

Grant Development Group Dynamics

Along with the concrete roles identified above, some less tangible roles will also be at play within the grant team. The interplay of people jockeying to claim various roles within the team can be fascinating to observe. Though group dynamics can be difficult to control, the effective harnessing of individual talents can lead to productive work environments.

Here are some additional roles Stinson and Renninger have identified within grant development groups:

- leader—either formally appointed or self-anointed
- summarizer—clarifies and reviews decisions
- focuser—brings the group back to the topic or task at hand
- recorder—writes responses and keeps notes
- rewarder—praises members for contributions
- technologist—provides technical assistance during the meeting
- nurturer—brings coffee, suggests breaks
- timekeeper—keeps discussions within the selected time frame[4]

Librarians will be pleased to know that many of the personal traits that make for ideal group members are common among those in the profession. According to public policy professors Dorothy Norris-Tirrell and Joy A. Clay, these traits include

- competent, technical knowledge
- effective communication skills
- self-awareness
- optimism
- reality-based catalyst for action
- team player[5]

Along with these traits, participants should enter the collaborative venture with a mind-set that promotes creativity and innovation. Effective collaborations call for hopefulness, a multidimensional perspective, and a willingness to learn—all of which are (or should be) common among library professionals.[6]

Who Should Participate?

The fact that informal roles exist among group members can be a boon for libraries. Though the library representative may ostensibly be at the table to provide research assistance, he or she may end up fulfilling other roles within the group. For instance, from several group experiences I realize that I am by nature a focuser. I refocus the group when discussions wander from the point at hand (which they do incessantly). I also often act as a summarizer, clarifying decisions that have been reached but lost as the discussion moves on. I have been able to exploit this combination of roles to benefit the grant and the library.

To take advantage of role opportunities, select individuals with the right kind of personality. No stereotypical quiet librarians should be designated to participate in grant design teams. Though studious researcher types are invaluable for gathering data (as discussed in the next chapter), these are not the types of people best suited for grant groups.

Early in my grant-writing career, I appointed the wrong type of person to participate in a grant team. Because she possessed outstanding research abilities, I invited a reference librarian to attend a grant development team meeting. Along with presenting her research findings, I was hoping she would explore other avenues for library participation during the meeting.

"Feel free to interject the library into the project whenever and wherever possible," I instructed. "Or, as I always tell my daughter, 'Use your big mouth, and speak up.'"

Despite my directive, I later learned that she had not uttered one word during the entire meeting. Even her research data went overlooked because she was too timid to bring it up.

Not only should the individual be prepared to speak up, she must also be "tactfully pushy." By that I mean she should be ready to insert the library into the project under development *forcefully and diplomatically* whenever the opportunity arises.

The types of library services and resources that could be suggested are discussed in chapters 6 and 7. But for now it should be kept in mind that the person at the table should be brazen enough to propose library support throughout the development project.

I did this so often in one grant team, it became an inside joke. "I hate to sound like a broken record," I would say, "but don't forget to include library materials in the budget." My incessant reminder paid off. More than $75,000 in library resources were included in the final grant budget.

Along with an outspoken personality, another factor to consider when inviting a library representative to the grant table is his or her own desire to be included. Appointment to a grant design team will translate into additional work. Lots of work. There will be meetings to attend, data to gather, documents to review, budgets to prepare, and sections of the proposal to write. If the library representative is less than enthusiastic about the project, resentment and frustration are almost sure to follow. Make sure you have what business experts call "commitment, not compliance" from the person chosen. Buy-in from the designated individual is vital.

All appropriate administrators must also be on board. Everyone needs to know that the supervisor *and* those above that person support the expenditure of time. Both the motivation of the individual, along with support of the supervisor, are required for library grant collaborative success. Tensions can arise if only one level supports grant activities. Often the upper echelons of administration will urge those below them to develop grants, while the rank-and-file supervisor is already overwhelmed with other duties. This was the case at one college where I worked. Though she never directly stated I should not develop grants, I knew my supervisor's support was halfhearted at best. I waited for her to retire before participating in grant development activities.

Once the participants have been finalized, their names should be widely disseminated. Other staff will need to assume the burden of additional work, so they should be forewarned. To ease the burden of the additional assignment, an explanation of the benefits that will accrue to the entire library—and library staff—should accompany the announcement. This will help remove—or at least reduce—resentment caused by a required workload shift.

At the Grant Development Table

If you followed the instructions above and managed to get a library person involved in someone else's grant project, give yourself a hearty congratulations. As I mentioned in the opening chapter, even if no money or resources are allocated, the library accrues benefits by simply being involved in collaborative projects. The library will profit through future collaborations, improved cross-organizational communications, and increased publicity.

But along with these advantages, you might as well try for financial support for the library. See chapter 6 for some of the specific items that the library might ask for. No matter what you try to obtain through the collaboration, it is important to come prepared with a wish list.

The late ALA lobbyist Eileen Cooke was fond of saying, "Never go to Capitol Hill without a bill in your back pocket. You never know when events will turn." The same is true in the world of grant development. At the last minute "events may turn" in favor of the library. Be prepared to seize such moments.

In one project I was involved in, the budget being developed still had money remaining after all the proposed activities had been funded.

"We need a children's room in the library," I said.

"How much would that cost?" I was asked.

I froze, then admitted, "I have no idea."

"We need a multimedia room in the day-care center," interjected the preschool director. Off the conversation went to computer projector prices and installation costs. If I had been prepared with hard numbers, we would have been talking about a library children's room instead of a day-care center multimedia room.

I vowed never to let this happen again. Though I lost out on that opportunity, I immediately began gathering numbers for next time. I assembled floor plans, furniture selections, and—most important—cost estimates. Next time I would have my numbers in my back pocket.

INDIVIDUAL GRANT DEVELOPERS

Though most grants are developed by groups, sometimes they are produced by individuals. These solo acts are most often performed by someone directly involved in the project or by a professional grant writer. From the library perspective, it will be easier to insinuate the library into a grant developed in a group setting. But individually created projects may also present opportunities for library collaboration.

In other words, it is tricky but not impossible to wrangle the library into someone's self-produced project. The key to success lies in the ability to identify the project being developed.

Chapter 3 discusses specific strategies for locating grant writers, but finding an individual who is developing her own grant is in fact often a matter of happenstance. Overheard conversations, reference desk interactions, or pre-meeting chitchat—any of these may lead to information about an individual grant developer. Never underestimate the power of plain-old gossip for this purpose. (See the discussion in chapter 3 on vendors for exploiting this intelligence source!)

When a grant developer is identified, you can ask her what projects she is working on and can talk about, keeping in mind the parameters of confidentiality mentioned earlier. Try to be open, creative, and innovative as you hear about any developing projects. Somewhere, somehow, there may be an angle for library inclusion.

THE TIME CRUNCH OF GRANTS

Whether you are working with an individual or with a grant team, it is vital to have your information available on a moment's notice. Grants are written within extremely tight time constraints. Though last-minute grant preparation is repeatedly disparaged by both funding agencies and professional grant developers, it happens more often than anyone likes to admit. In the opinion of one grant professional, the success of a proposal hinges more on program planning than on good writing. As Stephen Seward puts it, "Your results will improve dramatically if you take the time to think through your project in advance of sitting down to write your proposal."[7] But to effectively plan any project, you need time. Lots of time.

Unfortunately, time frames for developing grants have become even more abbreviated with the release of stimulus funds and other federal projects. Often the turnaround time between grant announcement and due date is so short, grant developers have little to no wiggle room. The moment the RFP is announced, the team or grant writer must immediately begin gathering data, creating projects, and developing budgets. To craft a winning proposal, the group or writer must do it NOW.

To interject anything into a developing grant, the library participant must be prepared to slap down a completed program, service, or library collection proposal right then and there. Likewise, if asked to locate data, the library must be able to produce the information instantly on demand.

I once attended a grant development meeting on the Friday afternoon before I was to leave for a week's vacation. When asked to prepare employment statistics for inclusion in the proposal, I agreed, but explained, "I'll be on vacation next week, so I'll get those to you in two weeks." Silence followed.

"Isn't there any way to get it now?" asked the team leader.

"I guess so," I said.

So instead of heading to my car, I hurried to the library reference desk. The unfortunate librarian scheduled for that Friday afternoon ended up with a last-minute research assignment. As I suggested earlier, it is a good idea to spread the word about potential grant development to everyone in the library. You never know who will end up getting extra work out of the endeavor.

NOTES

1. Karen Stinson and Phyl Renninger, *Collaboration in Grant Development and Management* (Washington, DC: Thompson Publishing Group, 2007), 85.

2. Ibid., 86.

3. Ibid., 86.

4. Ibid., 73.

5. Dorothy Norris-Tirrell and Joy A. Clay, *Strategic Collaboration in Public and Nonprofit Administration* (New York: CRC Press, 2010), 91.

6. Ibid., 86.

7. As quoted in Judith B. Margolin and Gail T. Lubin, eds., *The Foundation Center's Guide to Winning Proposals II* (New York: Foundation Center, 2005), vii.

5

RESEARCH—

THE LIBRARIAN'S SECRET WEAPON

Partnerships are in vogue in the nonprofit world. Breaking down the silos of individual organizations and departments has become the trend for projects ranging from health care to humanities. Everyone, it appears, wants to climb aboard the bandwagon and collaborate across institutions.

But collaboration is not simply a fad, like leisure suits or bell-bottom pants, that will soon go out of fashion. Behind the clamor for collaboration lies a legitimate reason for groups to work together. In an effective partnership, all groups involved benefit from each other. Organizational expert Jay Conrad Levinson calls it the "concierge approach," in which relationships are strengthened by each one "offering information, services, and access" to the others.[1]

As librarian-author Marylaine Block puts it, partnerships enable organizations to "combine their own staff's unique strengths and talents with those of other organizations,"[2] thereby benefiting all.

UNIQUE ABILITIES OF LIBRARIES

Libraries bring special strengths to grant collaborations. Librarians sometimes underestimate the power that flows from their unique position. First, libraries enjoy widespread communal admiration. As Block puts it, they generally have "the respect and good will [of] the community."[3] Janet L. Crowther and Barry Trott agree: "One resource that almost all libraries can count on is a sense of trust from their communities."[4]

Along with a reputation of respect, libraries have an expansive reach. As Block reminds us, libraries possess a "unique ability to reach every segment of the population."[5] And—in what I call the *secret weapon* of the profession—libraries can research just about anything. Through their special brand, libraries bring to potential partners much-needed subject expertise and information skills.

DEARTH OF RESEARCH ABILITIES

The ability to conduct research is especially valuable because so many lack this skill. As any librarian who deals with young people knows, the next generation can proficiently text and surf the net, but their research skills are nil. Likewise, within the grant-seeking world, some grant professionals—whether young or old—lack basic research abilities.

Even the professional literature on the topic leaves much to be desired. In the book *Writing for a Good Cause,* grant writers are directed to "do a World Wide Web search on your topic," where you will "find background material on your general topic—very helpful if you're writing about a subject you don't know well."[6]

That's it? Go to the web and search your subject? Granted (no pun intended), the World Wide Web can be a resource for researching grants, but it would hardly be the only source recommended by librarians.

I was appalled at one grant workshop when the presenter shared his strategy for locating a grant. He went to Yahoo! (his favorite search engine, he confided) and typed in "find grant." Then he eagerly proceeded to click on the first ten of 341,731 hits he retrieved.

Some professional grant literature does direct researchers to the library but provides no more direction than to "consult a librarian." One source suggests, "Collect more background material than you think you will need," but offers no further guidance on how to go about doing so.[7]

OVERVIEW OF RESEARCH NEEDED BY GRANT DEVELOPERS

Libraries stand to benefit from the inability of others to research. An effectively researched and data-supported grant proposal can produce exceptional results, while one lacking in supporting information can be discounted or disqualified from further consideration.

The two most potent areas for library-based research are (1) finding a grant and (2) locating background data to support the needs statement. Let's look at both of these areas in more detail.

Locating Grant Sources

Obviously, one of the first steps to submitting a grant proposal is finding an opportunity for funding. As one fundraising manual puts it, what you are looking for is a source "with a track record of giving to similar projects. The more closely a donor relates to your organization's . . . objectives," the more likely you are to be funded.[8]

As discussed in chapter 2, the major types of grants are government grants (federal, state, or local), corporate grants, foundation grants, and private or individual grants.

Grant opportunities in each of these categories will be found through a variety of online and print resources. Many of the online resources are available for free, while others are fee-based. Below is an overview of several of the most popular, comprehensive online grant resources. The bibliography provides other sources of information on grants. Grant-writing manuals also include listings of grant databases. And professional grant writers may be willing to share their favorite grant-finding resources upon request.

Grants Databases

GRANTS.GOV

Grants.gov is a foundational, consolidated government resource that searches more than $400 billion in federal grants. Here, seekers can locate discretionary grants offered by twenty-six federal grant-making agencies. Searching this site can be done without registering, but submitting a grant online does require advance registration. Beware, registering and uploading grants can be extremely time-consuming and frustrating. Allow at least three to five days simply to register.

CATALOG OF FEDERAL DOMESTIC ASSISTANCE (CFDA)

CFDA.gov has replaced what was at one time a standard print directory. It provides access to a database of all federal programs available to governmental bodies, public, private, and nonprofit organizations, special groups, and individuals. The online resource is searchable by agency, type of assistance, and eligibility. Grants to institutions and support to individuals are included.

FEDERAL REGISTER

The Federal Register is the official publication of rules and notices of federal funding. Published by the Office of the Federal Register, National Archives and Records Administration, this bible of grants announcements provides details about grant opportunities, along with contact information from the funding agency. Grant seekers rely on this resource to find announcements of agency RFPs. It is available online through the website of the Government Printing Office.[9]

FOUNDATION DIRECTORY ONLINE AND FOUNDATION GRANTS TO INDIVIDUALS ONLINE

The Foundation Center makes available two comprehensive databases through their network of Cooperating Collections.[10] One provides information on grants to organizations and the other lists sources for individuals. See chapter 3 for more information on these databases.

GRANTSTATION

GrantStation.com is a comprehensive database of foundations, international giving, and federal grants. Federal grants are displayed by date of funds available. International grants are searchable by country. Members of the national Grant Professionals Association (GPA) (discussed in chapter 3) are provided access to this database with membership.

GRANTNAVIGATOR PARTNERSHIP EDITION (PE)

GrantNavigator PE, provided by AFI (American Funding Innovators), is available to professional and municipal organizations.[11] U.S. federal agency funding opportunities are included and can be searched by agency name. GPA members are also provided access to this online resource through their membership.

GRANTSALERT

Founded in 1996 by a former high school social studies teacher, GrantsAlert.com specializes in school and teacher grants. Free access to announcements of corporate, foundation, state, and federal funding opportunities for education are included. Links are also provided for grant searching in other fields and for small businesses.

GUIDESTAR

GuideStar.org gathers and publicizes information about nonprofit organizations, philanthropic institutions, and charities. Though not a grants database per se, GuideStar is a free resource for organizations to share information about their missions, programs, accomplishments, and needs. Since many groups publicize their grants through the information provided at this site, it may prove valuable for grant seekers.

USA GOVERNMENT GRANTS

USA Government Grants lists grants by topic.[12] Housing, college scholarships, and personal grants are among the subject headings. Other databases are more comprehensive, but this resource may unveil additional opportunities.

Grant Directories and Listings

Another source of ideas for grant opportunities is the nonprofit literature. One key publisher for nonprofits is LRP Publications.[13] Among the titles they produce are

> *Corporate Philanthropy Report*
> *Education Grants Alert*
> *Federal Grants and Contracts Weekly*
> *Foundation and Corporate Grants Alert*
> *Health Grants & Contracts Weekly* [14]

Locating Previous Grant Proposals

One of the most important steps in identifying a grant opportunity is reviewing previously funded projects. The section above on locating grant sources provided information on how to explore this avenue. Though many funders change the focus of their giving from year to year, grant seekers can gauge the types of activities favored for support by studying the agency's past giving. Most of the databases above either provide, or lead to, archived information about previous funding. Depending on the project and institution, it may be helpful to contact the organization that won a previous grant. If appropriate, they may be able to offer suggestions on how to craft the proposal you are considering.

However, beware that the organization you approach may be applying for the new round of funding you are asking about. In other words, you may inadvertently be speaking to a potential grant competitor.

Locating Research to Support the Needs Statement

Along with the ability to locate grant opportunities through the resources above, librarians can dazzle grant developers by locating information to support the grant's needs statement. No matter the amount of the request, all funders need to be convinced that a need exists for the proposed project.

The needs statement is so central to grant requests, it is often one of the first—and most important—requirements of the proposal. As shown in the U.S. Department of Education STEM (science, technology, engineering and math) grant example below, demonstrating the need is afforded more weight in the grant reviewing process than any other area.

> *From criteria for a federal education grant proposal—*
>
> 1. Need for project, 20 points
> 2. Quality of project design, 15 points
> 3. Quality of project services, 15 points
> 4. Quality of project personnel, 10 points
> 5. Adequacy of resources, 10 points
> 6. Quality of management plan, 15 points
> 7. Quality of project evaluation plan, 15 points.[15]

To assist grant developers in crafting a needs statement, librarians need a clear understanding of the data sought. That knowledge will come by analyzing the RFP. Note what specific information is required. Does it call for a literature review, statistics, evidence-based outcomes?

Usually, the needs section of the document will specify the type of information that must be submitted in the proposal.

> *From criteria for a federal economic development grant—*
>
> Applicant must present socio-economic profile of the service area that is compelling (*facts & figures*), educational attainment, poverty, unemployment . . .
>
> *From criteria for a federal education grant—*
>
> Include articles, books, reports, studies showing the depth of the problem.
>
> *From criteria for a state workforce development grant—*
>
> Indicate average starting wage for graduates and the types of jobs requiring this degree.

In addition to these specifics, one grant-writing book suggests the needs section should include "nuggets . . . details or descriptions that arrest the reader." In order to make the case convincingly, it should include "vivid or memorable facts."[16]

Of course, it will help to have a clear understanding of the project as a whole. Coming to the search with a thorough understanding of the need to be met—and the proposed project to solve it—should inform and enhance the research quest.

Examples of Data Needed

The following examples describe several types of library research conducted for grants I helped develop. As you review the list, try to think of sources available through your library that would fulfill these requests.

Grant topic—economic development of a blighted area

To demonstrate the dire plight of an inner-city area, research demographic data on the residents of a one-mile area. Provide statistics about age, gender, race, education level, and income.

Grant topic—career development for job placement

To prove that graduates of a job development program would be able to secure employment, conduct research to find the average wages in a given field in our state. Produce trends showing that these wages have increased over last five years.

Grant topic—after-school tutoring

To show the need for a new after-school tutoring program, research academic performance on standardized tests in the local school system. Include the percentage of students failing English, math, and the overall test.

SUBJECT EXPERT VERSUS LIBRARY RESEARCHER

Once you have a handle on the type of information needed, there is still the question of who will conduct the research.

It may seem like a given by now that a librarian would be the one to conduct the required research. Others on the team, however, may assume that the subject expert on the team could produce the information needed. One book on grant development simply assumes that the mental health provider on a grant development team would be the one to gather statistics on children with mental health issues.[17] If the librarian wants to conduct the research, he or she must be prepared to speak up, but the offer would need to be made tactfully. Deferring to the expertise of the other team member, the librarian could say something like, "I'm sure Susan would be able to find this, but I know of an excellent resource for this information." Susan may be more than happy to delegate that portion of the work to the library.

If the library is successful in claiming the research role, it will need to be decided who in the library will undertake the task. The person selected will depend on the sensitivity of the topic, research competence level, and subject knowledge of the library representative on the grant team. As mentioned earlier, confidentiality is required while grants are in development to avoid tipping off possible competitors for the grant funds. Depending on the trustworthiness of the potential researcher, it may be advisable for the grant team member to simply conduct the research herself. However, if someone else possesses greater reference skills or knowledge of the subject, it may be best to have that person do the research instead. Whoever takes on this responsibility, it is essential to remember that, along with confidentiality, timeliness is crucial. Adequate research done on time is better than an excellent job done too late.

PRESENTING THE INFORMATION

Research results need to be presented in an easy-to-read format. Quotations should be clearly indicated, as should the sources of any data. Charts, graphs, and other visual representations of data can make a powerful case to demonstrate a grant need. Maps produced with GIS (geographic information system) technologies can be particularly helpful. To demonstrate the need for a new library branch, one library system produced a map showing the location of library card holders overlaid by a map of existing outlets. The need for new branches in certain locations was evident at a glance.

DON'T OVERDO IT

"Need Nelly" is the disparaging moniker grant experts Karen Stinson and Phyl Renninger assign to the grant team member who goes overboard with data. As they explain it, this type of individual "sends more information than you need, inundating the grant compiler with tons of information: website links, references, books and manuals."[18] I identify with this characterization, having exhibited this behavior more than once myself. Perhaps it is an occupational fault among librarians. We just never seem to think we have found enough information. There is always one more citation or one more article that will fill the bill. As you forward information, try to remember that less is more. A few pithy quotes or on-target statistics will be far more appreciated than reams of data.

NOTES

1. Jay Conrad Levinson, Rick Frishman, and Jill Lublin, *Guerrilla Publicity: Hundreds of Sure-Fire Tactics to Get Maximum Sales for Minimum Dollars* (Avon, MA: Adams Media, 2002), 24.

2. Marylaine Block, *The Thriving Library: Successful Strategies for Challenging Times* (Medford, NJ: Information Today, 2007), 49.

3. Ibid., 52.

4. Janet L. Crowther and Barry Trott, *Partnering with Purpose: A Guide to Strategic Partnership Development for Libraries and Other Organizations* (Westport, CT: Libraries Unlimited, 2004), 35.

5. Block, 52.

6. Joseph Barbato and Danielle S. Furlich, *Writing for a Good Cause: The Complete Guide to Crafting Proposals and Other Persuasive Pieces for Nonprofits* (New York: Simon and Schuster, 2000), 74.

7. Ibid., 74.

8. Smith, Bucklin & Associates, Inc., *Complete Guide to Nonprofit Management,* 2nd ed., ed. Robert H. Wilbur (New York: John Wiley & Sons, 2000), 117.

9. See http://www.gpo.gov/fdsys/.

10. See http://foundationcenter.org/collections/.

11. See http://www.afisystems.com/products.html.

12. See http://www.usagovernmentgrants.org/Government_Grants.html.

13. See http://www.lrp.com/.

14. Entrepreneur Press and Preethi Burkholder, *Start Your Own Grant-Writing Business* (New York: Entrepreneur Press, 2008), 32–33.

15. Application, Hispanic-Serving Institutions STEM and Articulation Programs, 2010, U.S. Department of Education, Office of Postsecondary Education.

16. Barbato and Furlich, 73.

17. Karen Stinson and Phyl Renninger, *Collaboration in Grant Development and Management* (Washington, DC: Thompson Publishing Group, 2007), 204.

18. Ibid., 20.

6

INCORPORATING THE LIBRARY
INTO GRANT PROPOSALS

f you have followed the advice so far, you have gotten yourself—or someone from the library—a seat at the grant table. Once again, congratulations for getting this far. Even if you do not garner one cent, the library has already benefited from the collaboration. Future projects may develop, which could lead to funds down the road. The cooperating institution now has a friendly face to call upon in the library. And the library, too, has found a valuable new contact.

But let's not play Pollyanna here. Informal contacts and future funds are always welcome. Cold hard cash is what you are after. So while at the grant table, there's no harm in asking for library support, assuming it is done diplomatically and at the right moment.

BEFORE THE ASK

Before you get to the asking part, keep in mind the following pre-grant-table guidelines.

Establish Pre-Grant Parameters

One of the biggest reasons librarians don't participate in grant activities is fear. Not only is there fear of failure but also consternation as to whether success will improve the financial situation of the library. As one source bluntly puts it, librarians are afraid "the money will be taken away."[1] This trepidation does not stem only from a pessimistic attitude but, sadly, from reality. This unhappy turn of events is common. Library budgets are sometimes reduced by the amount of new funds awarded.

To avoid falling victim to this reality, the issue should be raised before the grant effort commences. From the appropriate authorities—municipal financial officials, board members, or high-level supervisors—obtain a commitment that no deductions will be made from the library budget should the grant effort be successful. And get it in writing.

Come Prepared

As previously discussed, the library representative should come to the table prepared with an idea of what to ask for. Study the grant RFP for a vision of how the library could be involved—and receive funds for participating. Prepare a wish list based on that vision. Once you are at the table—and ideas begin flying about what the grant will include—it is too late to research prices. Know beforehand what the library needs and how much it will cost.

Authority of Library Representative

Make sure the representative has the knowledge, ability, and authority to insert the library into the project. It does no good to have the librarian say, "How about if the library offers a program on childhood obesity," unless that person is in a position to know the library can and will offer such a service. No one will benefit—and the library will lose credibility—if an idea is proposed and adopted but subsequently squashed by higher-ups in the library.

As mentioned in earlier chapters, the person at the table must possess the kind of personality that allows her to speak up. A withering librarian who is an excellent researcher, but introverted and shy, will do the library no good. The library representative should be an active participant and be able to make decisions about library involvement in the evolving project.

WHEN AND HOW TO ASK

When is it appropriate to ask for library funds? Only the person at the table can answer that. Knowing how to ask for library funds, along with knowing when, will depend on the situation. If the advice about envisioning library participation in advance was heeded, the person at the table should have a vision of a library activity to explain. Various methods exist to explain the idea and request its inclusion in the final proposal.

For instance, if the library is participating with a hospital on an immigrant population health awareness project, the library representative could propose a library collection of materials on health and wellness in the language of that group. One method would be to discuss the idea before the meeting, perhaps when the invitation to participate is extended. Especially if the person doing the inviting is the one initiating the grant, it would be appropriate to float the idea to that person prior to the first gathering. That way, the grant initiator will have had an opportunity to think about the idea. The librarian will also have had an opportunity to sense the initial reaction elicited by the idea.

Or, the library representative may decide to keep the idea close to the vest, unveiling it when she feels the time is right. From previous grant teams I have participated on, I can say that the most opportune moments have occurred either when the project activities were being developed or when the budget was discussed. That said, there is no hard-and-fast-rule as to when is best.

In one project I participated on, I was able to insert a library component into nearly every activity being planned. But for another project, I failed to imagine or insert library participation into even one grant activity. When the budget was being finalized, I half-heartedly asked, "Could we include some library materials if there is any money left?" A small amount of funds did remain, which were added to the budget with a general explanation of "library support," but I knew this addition did not enhance the grant (and may have detracted from it), since the funds were not tied to grant activity. Looking back, I'm still glad I tried. Neither I nor the library lost anything by my last-minute attempt to grab some money. Quite the contrary, I think some people in the room were even impressed to see such positive advocacy by a librarian. But I can imagine different circumstances, with different people at the table, where such a request could have been detrimental. As I mentioned earlier, the only one who can decide if and when to ask is the person in the room.

The person in the room will also need to be savvy enough to know when a change is needed. Many groups gather with the intent of creating one type of project, only to change direction dramatically. Sometimes new information necessitates making alterations. But more often than not, it is the personalities and persuasive abilities of those in the room that result in last-minute changes to the plan. The library representative must be ready to react to modifications of the project with appropriately altered library activities.

VOLUNTEERING FOR BUDGET DUTY

In some grant design teams, an individual or group is selected to prepare the budget and present the final document back to the group. Volunteering for the budget development team—or crafting the entire budget singlehandedly—presents an excellent opportunity to insert library funding. Without any fanfare, the budget could just happen to include a line item of $49,988 for library support (which always looks better than a round number such as $50,000).

WHAT TO ASK FOR

Three basic types of support are usually included in grant budgets.

- direct support
- indirect support
- in-kind contributions

The first two categories are discussed here. In-kind contributions are taken up in the next chapter.

Direct Support

When funds are allocated for library support—either through specific line items or to the library general fund—it is referred to as direct support. Suggestions for inclusion are listed below, but these should be viewed strictly as that—suggestions. If your library has a need for other items, services, or programs, by all means consider incorporating those requests into the developing project.

Good Old Money

In the best of all possible worlds, the library would receive unrestricted funds to use as the library sees fit. "Library support" would be the description in the budget narrative, perhaps with an explanation of how the library and program would be improved through the new monies. Depending on the grant and proposed project, such a vague line item may be good enough to warrant support. But most grants require—and the proposals would be stronger—if the specific library uses were stipulated. Ideas for these types of inclusions follow.

Library Materials

No matter the topic of the grant being addressed, a line item for more books for the library will almost always be appropriate. Unfortunately, institutions often overlook the library when beginning something new. "How many new programs have been established in colleges and schools without adequate provision for support materials?" ask the authors of one academic library fund-raising book. Grant proposals developed by colleges, university, or schools "should have a materials/equipment component built in for the library."[2]

If the grant requirements allow, it is generally to the library's advantage to leave the subject matter for the library materials unstated. A statement that funds will be used "to improve the library collection," instead of "for children's fairy tales," would allow the library to allocate the money at its discretion. However, most often the proposal itself will be strengthened by specifying the subject area. If the grant is offered to prepare future teachers, the proposal could simply state "for education materials." But the proposal would be stronger if it stated that the collection would be "for materials on teacher training." You may be able to get away with "the library collection on arts and humanities will be enhanced and expanded" in a humanities grant. But as a general rule, the more detail provided on the subject area, the better.

But beware that though the grant will be improved, the restrictive language will also limit library selection. The library will be bound by whatever collection content is stated. If the grant says funds will be used for books on animals, don't expect to buy more travel books. (But you might be able to get away with books on the flora and fauna of Hawaii.)

Nor should you forget that library materials consist of more than printed books. Multimedia resources, including DVDs and online resources, could also be requested for the given subject. Provisions for e-books and online databases could also be included. And consider print periodicals, which are still popular for casual reading and in-library browsing. It's conceivable that a special library collection could include all of the above. And don't forget furniture and equipment, as discussed below.

Library Shelving

Library shelving is an easy item to justify because everyone understands that if new books are coming to the library, they will need to physically be placed somewhere. Estimates of the costs for shelving ranges with book capacity will gladly be provided by shelving vendors. However, a request for new shelving assumes the library has some space to put it.

If the library doesn't have space, consider asking for remodeling to make space—or even asking for a new library! But don't get carried away. A grant with a maximum award of $50,000 cannot include a line item for a new library. But one for several million dollars, with capital improvements as one of the allowable expenses, could possibly encompass part of a library renovation.

Display cases for DVDs or magazine racks could also be included in the budget to house the items being purchased. Security cases—or even a security system—could be integrated into the grant budget, depending on the parameters of the RFP.

Library Material Processing

The costs for processing library materials, unlike those for books and shelving, are not generally understood by nonlibrarians. But these costs can be justified if team members and grant readers are provided with the appropriate information. Costs such as per item cataloging fees or binding charges could be provided. Once these processes are understood, you may be able to slip in requests for a new label maker or processing supplies. Additional staff to handle the acquiring, cataloging, processing, and shelving could also be justified as discussed below.

Library Staff

Just about anything you do through the grant will need staff. If more materials will be coming, someone will need to order them, catalog them, process them, and shelve them. I worked on one grant project for a day-care center that had a library with a sizable collection of teaching materials. But the collection was a librarian's nightmare. Books were piled randomly on the floor or shoved into makeshift shelving. In the collaborative proposal, rather than requesting new materials, funds for a part-time librarian to catalog and process the collection were included. This staffing request actually strengthened the proposal because this partnership would allow existing resources to be used more effectively.

Depending on the grant, full-time or part-time library staff may be permissible, paid either through a set salary or an hourly rate. Employee benefits should be calculated based on the existing rates of the hiring institutions or according to grant parameters. If allowed, having the library as the hiring agent is the easiest method for adding library staff. But if the grant or requesting organization does not allow for such an arrangement, the new personnel may need to be hired directly by the grant-winning organization, with the library assisting with the recruitment and selection of library personnel. Another option would be to have the library hire the staff but be reimbursed through grant funds by the requesting organization.

Office Equipment and Travel

In today's work world, very few jobs do not need a computer and printer. One computer per new employee, with a shared printer, is usually a justifiable request. Office supplies and printing costs are likewise expected expenses. Provisions for travel to local meetings or participation in out-of-state meetings or conferences may be appropriate, depending on the project.

One science grant I worked on had a healthy travel budget but needed someone to do the traveling. (As discussed elsewhere, grant money should not go unspent.) The library was able to help spend that portion of the budget by sending a librarian to look at best-practice science libraries. The destination library was conveniently located in the city where the librarian's son was thinking of going to college. Combining a visit to the library and the potential college campus constituted a win-win situation.

Library Programs

Just like materials, a library program can be justified no matter what the grant topic. Panel presentations, lectures by experts, or children's activities are possible directions these programs could take. As suggested above, before library programs can be proposed, the associated costs will need to be known. Come to the table with estimates of how much speakers would need to be paid. Hidden costs such as room rental fees, security, or custodial help should also be considered. If allowable by the funder, food for participants could be requested. Don't forget any supplies that may be required for the event. For libraries lacking program space, maybe a renovation would be in order. See the section on library shelving, above, for renovation considerations.

Indirect Costs and Indirect Support

Indirect costs, also called overhead or administrative costs, refers to the amount of the grant intended to cover the cost for an institution to administer the grant. In many grants the indirect cost will be a predetermined percentage of the award or based on a previously determined formula.

Indirect support, on the other hand, refers to nonmonetary sources of support the library receives *from* the grant other than the direct awarding of money. (Support the library offers *to* the grant project, known as an in-kind contribution, is discussed in the next chapter.) One example of indirect support to the library would be if a nonprofit organization received a grant to hire a nutrition expert. Arranging for that person to conduct a library program on healthy eating would constitute indirect support to the library. No funds would be awarded to the library for this purpose, but neither would the library be obligated to pay for such assistance. Or perhaps this person could help develop the library collection in selected subject areas or conduct training for library staff on current trends in disseminating health information. In each of these examples, the library would benefit without receiving direct funding from the grant.

The library representative at the table should keep this type of support in mind, especially if direct funding of the library does not appear to be forthcoming. But indirect support should be considered a fallback position. Remember, cold hard cash is always preferable!

NOTES

1. Patricia Senn Breivik and E. Burr Gibson, "Operating within a Parent Institution," in *Funding Alternatives for Libraries*, ed. Breivik and Gibson (Chicago: American Library Association, 1979), 127.

2. Ibid., 125.

7

HOW THE LIBRARY CAN
SUPPORT GRANT PROJECTS

The previous chapter provided tips on finagling funds for library support into the developing grant projects of other organizations. But the library could also benefit by finessing itself into nonmonetary segments of the grant. Much like the adage one must give love to receive love, giving away library services may ultimately amass future library support. This chapter suggests some types of collaboration that could benefit the library now or in the future.

IN-KIND CONTRIBUTIONS

In-kind contributions from the library are the opposite of support to the library. Instead of receiving support *from* the grant, the library would offer support *to* the grant. Many major grant projects require that a stated percentage of the budget be derived from in-kind sources. Unlike direct financial support, these contributions are usually estimates of contributed costs. For instance, if the library hosts a program for the grant but does not charge for the room, the actual (or estimated) cost for using that room for the duration could be calculated as an in-kind contribution from the library. The estimated staff time required to set up the room—administrative, custodial, or both—could be an in-kind contribution. If the library offered to conduct research for a project, the associated costs could be calculated.

Though it seems counterintuitive, the library benefits by offering these types of contributions to the project. Publicity and community support accrue to the library from the collaboration. At the same time, the project benefits through the positive public image of libraries. And in-kind contributions in one grant could lead to direct funding in a future one. Naturally, financial support to the library is preferred. But some participation is better than none. Providing in-kind contributions at least keeps the library at the grant table.

Providing Library Materials Support

As discussed in the previous chapter, virtually any topic could include support for new library materials. A job-training grant? Consider books on careers and vocational training. Childhood obesity? Request databases on psychology, child development, and physical education. A grant for biological research? Along with science resources, the library could obtain materials on how to write research reports (or how to improve writing in general). The applicability of libraries is universal to just about any project or program under consideration.

Ideally, the funds for materials in the appropriate subject area will be included in the grant proposal. If that is not possible, however, the library could participate as an in-kind contributor as mentioned above by dedicating a portion of its materials budget to the project under consideration. For instance, if the library usually spends $50,000 on print periodicals, it could designate 5 percent of that amount, or $2,500, to purchase subject-specific titles. Without spending any additional money, the library will be able to participate in the project and help meet the grant's in-kind requirement.

Evaluating the Program

Along with mandating cross-institutional partnerships, another major trend in grant awarding is the emphasis on assessment. At every phase of the project, the funders need assurance that the project is meeting its stated goals and funds are being used appropriately. Many large grants require an outside evaluator hired for this purpose. These individuals perform periodic reviews and audits and report their findings to the grant administrators.

However, smaller grants must rely on other methods of assessment. Sometimes this is accomplished through an internal review committee. Because this body is made up of individuals within the organization, it cannot conduct the same objective review as an outside evaluator. Nonetheless, internal groups can still play an important role in the assessment process by periodically asking if tasks are being accomplished on time and within budget.

Another way grants fulfill the evaluation requirement is through voluntary advisory councils (or committees). Usually made up of stakeholders in the project, these groups meet periodically throughout the grant cycle. Along with receiving reports on grant activities, advisory councils can make suggestions on solving problems or meeting project goals. Internal review committees do the same but usually consist only of stakeholders within the institution.

Internal review committees and advisory councils are excellent venues for library representation. Libraries enjoy a reputation for impartiality, rationality, and an openness to all opinions. These traits are perfectly suited for service on a grant assessment body. The grant writer would be wise to include a library representative on any appropriate evaluation structure being planned for the developing project.

Publicizing the Program

Just as a library's collection embraces all subject areas, the library itself reaches all segments of its community. No matter the type of library—public, academic, school, or special—every member of the service area comes in contact with the library. One former boss of mine would remind me of this every time we received a complaint about the library. "Get used to it. Remember back in high school. The school cafeteria and library were the only two places everybody went to, so they received the most complaints."

The upside of its ubiquity is the library's publicity potential. Because it touches every segment of the service area, the library is uniquely positioned to spread the word about new programs. Many grants—if not most—are awarded to organizations to begin something new. Ideally, the award will fund a new approach to solving a pressing problem. Though some grants support ongoing projects, many bestow funds on innovative methods to improve lives. Those whose lives are targeted for said improvement need to know about the proposed solution. Enter the library as the source of knowledge.

As was discussed in the section on grant components in chapter 2, most grant proposals require a plan for publicizing the project. Writing news releases, presenting at conferences, and submitting articles to professional journals are among the usual suspects included in the promotional activities. Disseminating information through the library would benefit the grant by offering a novel approach (no pun intended) to spreading the word about the project. The library would also profit by reminding those in its service area of the role it plays in dispensing information.

Depending on the requirements of the grant RFP, library publicity could count as an in-kind contribution. To translate the activity into a budget figure, an estimate of the cost of distributing the information could be calculated. For instance, if a direct-mail campaign usually costs $1.50 per person (which includes printing, mailing, and handling expenses), this figure would be multiplied by the number of those receiving the mailing. Or if a full-page announcement appears in a four-page library newsletter, one-fourth of the cost of that publication could be listed as an in-kind contribution.

Hosting the Program

Hosting a program initiated by the grant could potentially provide another avenue of support from the library. Complete sponsorship of the event, be it a panel presentation, lecture, or hands-on activity, would fit perfectly into the outreach mission of the library. On a more limited basis, the library could offer available meeting space for these events. Or the library could simply lend its name as a cosponsor of the event, again extending its community support through the association.

Providing Space

Speaking of offering space, if the library has any unused offices, they may consider housing the developing project. Especially with all the recent downsizing, spaces formerly occupied by laid-off librarians or outsourced services may be available. However, think carefully before making this offer. As they say in the military, "There is nothing as permanent as a temporary building." Once the space is occupied, it may prove difficult—if not impossible—to reclaim it for library purposes.

Spending Their Money

One final suggestion on how the library can collaborate on other people's grants is to offer to spend their recently received grant funds. Though it sounds self-serving (well, it *is* self-serving), the offer would also benefit the granting agency.

One of the dirty little secrets among grant administrators is that their success depends on them spending all their allotted funds. I call this money-spending directive secret because it is never stated outright in the proposal. Certainly, the organization receiving the funds must meet all the objectives of the grant, submit reports in a timely fashion, and assess the project in accordance with the grant. But allocating and spending all funds within the grant period is also vital for the success of the program (not to mention the continued employment of the grant administrator).

Few funding agency personnel wish to initiate the laborious process of reclaiming granted funds. Not only would the project be perceived as a failure, but the paperwork required to rescind and then reallocate grant funds would be cumbersome. To avoid this, grant administrators must find ways to spend all funds on purposes appropriate for the project within the allotted time period.

As anyone who has dealt with a budget knows, most budgets are estimates of anticipated expenditures. According to one standard dictionary, an estimate is "an approximate judgment or opinion." Even the most carefully researched budget proposal will contain figures that turn out to be incorrect. And even the most methodically planned projects will require last-minute changes. All of which can result in excess grant funds.

As has been mentioned several times in this and previous chapters, the library is perfectly poised to serve the grant—no matter what the subject area—through the library collection. Allocating funds for library materials can be justified by identifying a subject matter central to the project. Spending funds in this manner will enhance the project while improving the library collection and serving its users.

But another hidden benefit of spending money on library materials is that it provides a last-minute method to encumber and spend funds quickly. Most libraries use book vendors that allow blanket orders to be placed without specifying titles. One major book distributor even sends out e-mails at the end of the fiscal year with this in mind. "As the fiscal year-end approaches, we would like to remind you that . . . [we] will gladly set up a deposit account for any funds you need to have encumbered."[1] The vendors and library administrators know that with just one completed form or budget transfer, thousands of dollars can be committed within minutes.

For grant administrators who discover last-minute unexpended funds—which happens all the time—nick-of-time expenses can be a lifesaver. On several occasions I have been able to exploit this to the benefit of the library and grant personnel. My offers of library expenditures made to grant administrators at the conclusion of their projects have been enthusiastically received. Rather than appearing as greedy and self-interested, these offers to spend funds quickly for a legitimate, grant-related purpose are seen as helpful.

To enable the grant administrator to easily take advantage of this possibility, however, the original proposal should include a line item for library materials. If library materials were not part of the original proposal, authorization for such an expense may need to be obtained from the funding agency. This could delay the budget process and defeat the purpose of providing a quick, last-minute solution for spending grant funds. To avoid this, try to have library funds included in the original grant proposal. To find out how to do this, see chapter 6.

Supporting the Project by Connecting Collaborative Partners

The ability to bring collaborative partners together is an untapped resource of the library. As I will discuss in more detail in the next chapter, more and more grants require organizations to collaborate with other groups to solve problems. Though an organization's personnel are well aware of the need for partners, they often have no clue how to go about finding one.

The library could play a pivotal role as a matchmaker for nonprofits. This linking service could be as informal as forwarding information about an emerging tutoring program to a club for retired teachers. Or it could be as elaborate as establishing a clearinghouse for nonprofits. No matter which route is taken, the library would benefit by serving as the conduit between the organizations.

Bringing the groups together also provides an opportunity for insinuating the library into the resulting grant. "Don't forget to include the library in your project!" could be jotted down on the slip of paper or included in the e-mail with the organization's contact information. Again, even if no direct funds result, community relations will be enhanced and future projects may develop.

NOTE

1. Renee Chastain, e-mail message to author, May 17, 2010.

8

PARTNERSHIPS
AND BEYOND

There are partnerships, and then there are partnerships. Sometimes "cooperating with an agency with which one is not immediately connected"—one definition of partnership—can amount to a true collaboration between organizations. But other times the arrangement can be the equivalent of an organizational hookup. It may be briefly satisfying for both parties, but it doesn't lead anywhere. For substantial and long-term financial success, libraries will want to consider a more permanent arrangement. This chapter discusses how a library can go beyond involvement in other organizations' grant initiatives to achieve more lasting relationships.

WHY COLLABORATE?

Metaphors abound in the grant literature to describe the cooperative arrangement between nonprofit organizations. Marriage is by far the most common reference, with dating, courtship, and engagement frequently thrown in for good measure.[1] The late library expert Kathleen de la Peña McCook imagined "a giant jigsaw puzzle. The pieces just need to be put in place."[2] Others borrow from the commercial world. "Think of your project as a good business run by co-owners."[3]

No matter how you envision it, the ultimate goal of the union is to benefit all parties. More and more grant opportunities are available only to two or more organizations working together. Just as they do with carpool lanes, governmental authorities are trying to entice cooperation.

But, as grant experts Karen Stinson and Phyl Renninger have noted, grant reviewers frequently turn down a request that includes partners but lacks collaboration. Especially through the budget, reviewers will detect what appear to be "purchased partnerships." The participating organizations may donate time or in-kind support (as discussed earlier), but the funding agency needs to see mutually beneficial relationships.[4]

Libraries are encouraged to seek partnerships for reasons beyond money (though money is still a valid motivator). Reciprocity is the ultimate objective, which has been defined as "mutual dependence where one group needs the other to be successful."[5] Graphically, the relationship can be depicted as intersecting circles, with the area of overlap as the collaborative opportunity.

Former St. Louis Public Library director Glen E. Holt explains that successful partnerships have at their hearts "joined self-interest." Each partner should "gain more by working with another than by working alone."[6] Howard County (MD) Library director Valerie J. Gross agrees. "Forging partnerships with community organizations leads to success that goes beyond the benefits to the participants in the joint programs."[7] Library expert Marylaine Block sees "shared purposes" as the ultimate goal.[8]

Another reason for working with outside organizations is the extra visibility that comes through the promotional possibilities presented by the partnership (how's that for alliteration). Gaining expertise from the partner is another benefit. The potential for consolidating a fragmented, cumbersome service into a single, streamlined procedure provides yet another benefit.

THE PUSH FOR PARTNERSHIPS

External forces are coalescing to encourage groups to work collaboratively. A seismic shift has occurred in the funding world, with joint projects favored over solo endeavors. At one time collaboration was required only for large national projects; smaller local efforts were spared the need to join together. Within the library world, grand initiatives such as OCLC and regional, multitype consortia always required multiple libraries, but local groups could go it alone.

As available funds have been reduced, funders now must leverage their limited resources through collaborative efficiencies on even the smallest level. In 2009, the Ford Foundation announced plans to spur collaboration among its grantees.[9] Even in the corporate world, a push is on to partner with nonprofit agencies. One recent example is the Disney Institute, where hospital health-care workers learned from Disney how to add the "nice" factor to patient care.[10]

Local governments have responded to the partnering push by creating departments dedicated to nurturing collaborative efforts. For example, since 2006, the mayor of Los Angeles supported the creation of a cabinet-level public liaison to the philanthropic community; the City of Newark, New Jersey, has established an Office of Philanthropic Liaison; and the City of San Francisco set up a Communities of Opportunity office.[11]

LIBRARIES AND COLLABORATION

Forming partnerships is nothing new for libraries. Working jointly has been part of the library landscape for years. Sarah Ann Long, then president of ALA, made "Libraries Build Community" her theme in 1999, calling on libraries to collaborate and form partnerships more than a decade ago. "What activities can you undertake that will build the community as a constituency for your library?" she asked. "With whom can you form an alliance? Who shares your goals?"[12]

As Janet L. Crowther and Barry Trott have since noted, however, "Libraries have been slow to pick up on the value and necessity of cross-sector partnering. Most libraries have not extended this model of collaboration beyond working in partnership with other libraries."[13] This is especially unfortunate now because the need for outside funds has only intensified the push for collaboration.

Where to Find Partners

Assuming you are convinced that genuine partnerships are the way to go, the next question becomes where to find one. Part of the answer can be found in chapter 3. As discussed there, grants are usually crafted by nonprofit agencies. By following the suggestions on how to find a grant-writing organization, you might also uncover organizations with whom the library could partner. In addition, libraries may want to consider the following for referrals to potential partners.

American Library Association

The national office of ALA fields thousands of calls from local and state organizations. Depending on the subject matter under consideration, the appropriate ALA office or bureau may be able to provide leads to organizations in your area.

Headquarters of Associations

In the United States, an association exists for virtually every profession, interest group, and topic imaginable. Finding the national or state headquarters for a given subject may yield information about organizations operating at the grassroots level.

Community Development Corps/Comprehensive Community Initiatives

The concept of civic engagement through community building evolved in the 1990s. To improve the quality of life in neighborhoods, many areas created comprehensive community initiatives as part of the broader community development corporation movement.[14] Libraries looking for organizations that are striving to improve the lives of residents may want to begin their quest here. Contacting the local planning council or United Way office may lead to a referral to entities operating in your locale.

How to Approach Potential Partners

For many librarians, cold-calling an agency to propose a partnership is dreaded as much as a trip to the dentist. For some, a root canal would be preferred. This reluctance to make the initial contact with potential partners is not restricted to the library profession. Many administrators of small nonprofits experience the same reluctance. One nonprofit agency administrator expressed her enthusiasm for a library-based nonprofit clearinghouse for this very reason. "So many people who work for small nonprofits are too intimidated to contact the director of some major organization. Using the library to help make those initial connections would really help."[15]

The following approaches may take some of the fear out of the initial call.

Start with the Organization's Library

"There's something I always wanted to know," said an airplane seatmate upon learning I was a librarian. "Do you get out of paying library fines? Is there professional courtesy among librarians so you don't charge each other?" Would that it were. Each time I shell out money for my overdue fines, I am reminded of that conversation. Though we don't excuse each other's late fees (though maybe we should), we do share an affinity for others in our profession. Librarians are comfortable talking to other librarians.

To take advantage of this professional connection, you could begin your search for a potential partner by contacting the agency's library. Larger organizations such as the United Way, hospitals, colleges, and schools frequently have a library or information center staffed by at least a part-time librarian.

As an example, let's say your library would like to propose partnering with an organization to offer a citizenship class in one of the branches that serves a large immigrant population. Instead of calling the United Way director, you could explain the idea to the organization's librarian. She could let you know of similar programs or the appropriate person within the organization to approach.

Make House Calls

If the organization is large enough to have a physical facility, you could drop in, scout around, and get a feel for the place. This would be especially valuable if you have a new service in mind that would need a base of operation. For instance, if you are thinking of extending library service to a new population, you may need to partner with an organization serving that demographic. Check out the places—and associations—frequented by the target audience to locate a base for the new program.

In our current security-conscious environment, this may not be appropriate for certain locations, such as schools or children's services. But some organizations, such as job centers, government buildings, and recreation centers, may lend themselves to meandering.

Contact Newly Appointed Officials

"A new broom sweeps clean," goes the adage. When a new administrator comes to an organization, he or she is often open to making his or her mark by initiating a new service or program. Watch for announcements of new appointees to organizations. Once the new person has settled in, introduce yourself and explain the basics of what the library offers. Then pitch your potential partnership.

Schedule a Meeting

Once you have identified the appropriate place, person, and project, you could suggest a meeting to discuss it further. Whether face-to-face, on the phone, or online, a prearranged meeting will allow for the time needed to explain the idea fully. Once the meeting is set, others from the library, the potential partner, or other agencies could be included.

Conduct a What's-Coming-Up Survey

If you have not zeroed in on a service or potential partner, it may be helpful to conduct a broad sweep of several organizations. The book *Partnering with a Purpose* suggests selecting a few community organizations and contacting them to see what plans they have in place for the coming year. You could tell them you are simply "gathering information that will shape the library's response to community trends." Make sure you explain the purpose of your inquiry, lest it appear that "the library is seeking to take ideas . . . rather than seeking to . . . collaborate."[16]

Finalizing and Formalizing the Partnership

Once an appropriate partner has been identified and the initial contact made, an exploration of joint projects or services comes next. A give-and-take between representatives from both organizations will—or should—ensue. Beware, though, that if one organization effortlessly obtains support for all activities proposed, something may be amiss. It may be an indication that the partnership is too one-sided. Though uncomfortable, disagreements may show true give-and-take among the partners. Don't think, on the other hand, that you need to encourage trouble. But you may want to take note if all is going too smoothly, lest it be a symptom of organizational inequality.

Once any imbalance is fixed, the next step is to formalize the joint arrangement. Those with authority to enter into joint initiatives will need to be included. Boards or high-level administrators may need to provide their imprimatur. Beware that many potential partnerships fall apart at this stage, as discussed below.

Once the appropriate approvals are obtained, the partnership will need to be formalized in writing. The format of such an agreement varies according to the partners and governing bodies. Sometimes it is accomplished through an agreement for services, which stipulates what the partner will perform and the amount of money to be paid. Other documents can include a formal letter of commitment, sometimes called an MOU, or memorandum of understanding. Common elements found in such a document include

- collaborative purpose
- structure
- participating individuals, with responsibility and obligations
- time frame
- financial and other commitments
- monitoring format[17]

Detailed budgets, with partner agency staff and related expenses delineated, frequently accompany the documentation. In some instances a formal contract will need to be drawn up.

Other formal agreements used in forming collaborations can include collaboration guidelines and participant agreements. Much like the MOUs, guidelines detail the group's mission, membership, governance, rule-making, and dissolution procedures. Participant agreements are intended for individuals to obligate themselves to actions needed by the group. These signed agreements can include pledges of what each person will be responsible for, the numbers of meetings they will attend, and the committees they will serve on.[18]

Applying for the Grant as a Partner

Just like in ballroom dancing, when applying for a grant one of the partners must lead and the other follow. Which group is chosen depends on the grant's eligibility requirements, the parameters of the project, each organization's experience administering grants, the size of the organizations involved, and the appropriateness of the project to each group's mission. Good old-fashioned politics can play a part, too, if one of the groups exerts its power to claim the lead role.

The partner chosen as the leader will serve as what is called the "primary fiscal agent," which is a fancy way of saying they get all the money. If the grant allows, the lead group may be entitled to keep a predetermined portion of the funds as *indirect costs* (as discussed in chapter 6), which are intended to reimburse the fiscal agent for the costs associated with administering the project.

Funds from the lead organization will be distributed to the participating partners through a variety of methods, depending on the restrictions set forth in the grant or collaboration documents. Sometimes the partners are allowed to receive money from the lead group as a subcontractor. In other arrangements, the lead organization may be able to hire employees of the partner organization on an adjunct or part-time basis, in which case the employees take on grant work in addition to their regular jobs. Still other methods include providing funds directly to the partner agency's program participants through scholarships, stipends, or grants to individuals.

No matter which method is used, the groups must comply with all financial regulations set forth by the lead organization and the granting agency. Detailed record-keeping must be maintained and provided for all internal and external audits which occur during the granting period.

Once it has been determined which group will serve as the lead, that group must assume responsibility for completing and submitting the grant proposal, while the partner is responsible for providing any required supplemental information or letters of support.

CAUTIONARY NOTES

The benefits of collaborating with a partner organization are many. However, as fitness trainers are fond of saying: no pain—no gain. Or to return to the marriage metaphor, couples need to constantly work on their relationship. And so it can be for nonprofit collaborations.

Unreal Expectations

In the words of a report from a nonprofit health-care group, some people believe "that collaboration will solve all of a community's problems." To avoid disappointment, the goal of the partnership should be agreed to—and clearly stated—at the beginning, middle, and end of the process. In other words, "clarify together what the goal of the collaboration will be," and remind the participants of this focused aim throughout the project development.[19]

Partnership Misfits

Partnerships must fit within an organization's mission, and they must be symbiotic—of mutual benefit to both parties. Differing organizational size may be a potential problem. Though some big fish/small fish arrangements benefit both, the differing sizes may be potentially hazardous if the smaller group is operating on a limited—a.k.a., shoestring—budget. Organizations with high turnover should also be avoided. Groups suffering from poor internal communication or unclear reporting structures could also be detrimental. Library director Valerie Gross (Howard County, MD) has declined several partnership opportunities for fear that they were potentially too one-sided, requiring "an imbalance of obligations and disproportionate benefits."[20]

Danger Points

One of the points where many cooperative arrangements deteriorate is at the formal approval point. People unfamiliar with the development of the project are often asked to approve an activity of which they have no prior knowledge. Though those at the grassroots level may be enthusiastic about the project, the benefits may not be apparent to higher-ups. To avoid this, remember to recite the pluses of the project when discussing it with superiors. Make sure any requests for formal approval are accompanied by a summary of advantages the library will gain, along with the description of the collaboration.

Another potential pitfall to avoid is crafting a written agreement with vague partner responsibilities. This document will need to contain sufficient specifics. As Patricia Senn Breivik and E. Burr Gibson noted more than thirty years ago, "Failure to establish agreed-to guidelines can lead to chaos and failure."[21]

Problems can also develop if one partner promises to perform certain actions but fails to deliver. This can be especially dire during the proposal development process if the partner does not deliver the needed information or support letters to the lead organization by the time the grant is due. Afterward, difficulties can ensue if the partner organization does not live up to expectations. Perhaps someone within the organization is opposed to the project. Or maybe the wrong group has been asked to participate. To once again return to the marriage analogy, at the conclusion of the project a divorce may be needed, so that both parties can move on and find the right partner next time.

Trust—the Final Requirement

If you are lucky enough to avoid most of the stumbling blocks mentioned above, the collaboration should be ready to roll. By finding and approaching appropriate partners and formalizing the relationship, you will begin to form a genuine collaborative arrangement. No matter the size of the collaborative project, trust is an essential element for success. Libraries are especially vulnerable because they enter the partnership with high levels of institutional trust by virtue of the organization. Block warns, however, that a partnership gone sour may put this trust in the library at risk.[22] A shared commitment to a common mission and follow-through on all promises are needed. But trust among the participants builds a solid foundation from which further collaborative activities can be launched.[23]

NOTES

1. Marylaine Block, *The Thriving Library: Successful Strategies for Challenging Times* (Medford, NJ: Information Today, 2007), 53; ibid., 8; Janet L. Crowther and Barry Trott, *Partnering with Purpose: A Guide to Strategic Partnership Development for Libraries and Other Organizations* (Westport, CT: Libraries Unlimited, 2004), 45.

2. Kathleen de la Peña McCook, *A Place at the Table: Participating in Community Building* (Chicago: American Library Association, 2000), 3.

3. Karen Stinson and Phyl Renninger, *Collaboration in Grant Development and Management* (Washington, DC: Thompson Publishing Group, 2007), 8.

4. Ibid., 8–9.

5. Ibid., 6.

6. As quoted in Crowther and Trott, 8.

7. As quoted in Block, 72.

8. Block, 64.

9. Ericka Harney, "Creating Impact with Policymakers: Cases of Building Cross-Sector Partnerships to Build Stronger Programs and Grant Applications," *Journal of the American Association of Grant Professionals* (Fall 2009): 17.

10. Andrew Doughman, "New Program Focuses on Health Care Workers," *Sun Sentinel*, July 19, 2011, 1D.

11. Harrney, 18–19.

12. As quoted in McCook, ix.

13. Crowther and Trott, 7.

14. McCook, 33.

15. L. Schotthoefer, personal communication, February 28, 2011.

16. Crowther and Trott, 59.

17. Dorothy Norris-Tirrell and Joy A. Clay, *Strategic Collaboration in Public and Nonprofit Administration* (New York: CRC Press, 2010), 85.

18. Ibid., 329–333.

19. *Improving Stakeholder Collaboration: A Special Report on the Evaluation of Community-Based Health Efforts*, Group Health Community Foundation, Seattle, WA, [2001], 14.

20. As quoted in Block, 72.

21. Patricia Senn Breivik and E. Burr Gibson, "Operating within a Parent Institution," in *Funding Alternatives for Libraries*, ed. Breivik and Gibson (Chicago: American Library Association, 1979), 125.

22. Block, 52.

23. McCook, 53.

GRANT-WRITING CAREERS

FOR LIBRARIANS

Now I understand why you are so involved in grants," said a fellow librarian. "It's really fun!"

Thus concluded my colleague after serving on her first grant team. Not only was she pleased that the grant development process had provided her with valuable knowledge and much-needed resources for the library; she actually had *fun* doing it! What a welcome change for librarians, who, given the current economic situation, rarely have the opportunity to enjoy their work these days.

My colleague's enthusiastic reaction to grant involvement was surprising to her but not to me. I have observed several librarians approach grant development with trepidation and anxiety only to find the experience enjoyable. Some librarians get so hooked on the process they search out another grant opportunity as soon as the first one ends. Others are so attracted to the field that, like me, they consider pursuing a career in grant development.

This chapter is directed at those librarians who find themselves so smitten with grant development they want more information on the grant profession. Along with a discussion of the affinity between librarians and grant professionals and the background of grant development careers, suggestions are provided on how to permanently craft a career combining librarianship with grant development.

SIMILAR SKILLS

If there is any truth to the saying that you like what you are good at, librarians should take an instant liking to grant development. The two fields require many of the same abilities. This overlap was revealed to me when I was asked to review candidates for positions in our college's grants office. The job descriptions for two grant positions—one for a grant writer and another for a grant research associate—included the following:

- ability to research and disseminate information
- ability to retrieve data and information from documents, the Internet, and databases

- ability to compile information and provide research support for a department
- possession of excellent research, verbal, and written communication skills

As I read these requirements, it dawned on me that a librarian would be an asset to the grant team. This realization was confirmed when I noticed that a master's in library science was one of the preferred degrees for both posts. Since then, I have found many job postings for grant-related jobs that include mention of the library degree. As I write this, one offer for a part-time position at a local nonprofit includes a note that "a librarian background would be a good fit."[1] One grant research assistant I know enrolled in library school after realizing the benefit of having expert research skills. Another grant professional plans to pursue a master's in library science in retirement; she hopes to use it to create her ideal retirement job combining libraries with grant development.

Most people think writing is the main skill required for grant development. But writing is only one facet of the process. Some would even argue that it is the least time-consuming aspect of grant work. Conducting research to find the best funding opportunity, locating data to support the need for a project, organizing information, and keeping track of proposals are all central to grant work. Most librarians can—or should—excel at all of these duties. Obviously, the ability to write effectively is an important skill for a grant developer. But even librarians who lack writing ability could contribute to an organization's resource development efforts.

SIMILAR CAREER PATHS

"What do you want to be when you grow up?" is almost never answered with, "A librarian." Studies have shown that few librarians contemplated a career in the field when they were young. The same is true for grant writers. Both occupations tend to attract adults, many of whom are pursuing second careers later in life. Many—if not most—grant professionals enter the field through grant-related responsibilities assumed in previous positions. One high-level grant executive I know started out with the Girl Scouts. Another colleague of mine who owns a grant-writing consulting firm began as a college English teacher. She had a U.S. Department of Education Title V grant dumped on her and, as the saying goes, the rest is history.

Because so many grant professionals enter the profession mid- and late-career, librarians should have no trouble pursuing a career in the field. As mentioned above, because they come equipped with so many of the requisite skills, librarians are attractive candidates for many positions in the grant world.

GRANT-WRITING CAREERS: AN OVERVIEW

Librarians considering a grant-writing career may want to know that initially, grant writing was a subset of fundraising. The broad field of bringing in money encompassed not only securing grants but such functions as soliciting major donations, alumni relations, planned giving, and prospect development. Spurred by the proliferation of government, corporate, and foundation grants, a specialization in the proposal development aspect of fundraising has emerged.

Those considering a career move that includes grant development have many places of employment to choose from. Many large organizations, such as hospitals, school systems, colleges, municipalities, and museums, maintain substantial grants departments. Smaller groups, such as environmental groups, faith-based organizations, and human services organizations, support only a small office. The larger organizations have staffs of several full- and part-time employees. Sometimes only one person, working full- or even part-time, is employed at the smaller agencies. Both small and large departments use outside grant developers to expand their grant-producing capacity. Many nonprofit organizations hire freelance grant professionals instead of maintaining any internal staff. Volunteers often take on the grant-writing role.

Expected Salary or Income

Anyone contemplating a career in grant writing should be aware that producing proposals on a commission basis is considered a violation of the profession's ethical standards. The Grant Professional Association's Code of Ethics states, "Members shall not accept or pay a finder's fee, commission, or percentage compensation based on grants and shall take care to discourage their organizations from making such payments. Compensation should not be written into grants unless allowed by the funder."[2]

Grant writers are most often employees of an organization or independent consultants. The 2010 salary survey conducted by the Grant Professionals Association found the average salary of grant professionals employed full-time to be $60,297, with pay ranging from $23,000 to $143,000. The part-time average rate is $28.62 per hour, with a range of $12–$60. The income of those working as consultants in the field was not stated, but 69 percent reported an increase in their net income when they became a consultant. Almost all consultants (95 percent) feel adequately compensated for their work, as do 76 percent of those employed as grant professionals.[3]

Another source found the average annual salary for the profession to be anywhere from $50,000 to $300,000 per year, with the average rate for beginning grant writers ranging from $40–$80 per hour.[4] Experienced writers can command $100 per hour or more. The per diem rate can range from $500 to $2,000, depending on expertise. Grant writers working on a per project basis are paid anywhere from $1,000 up, with many grant projects paying $10,000 per proposal.[5]

Full- and Part-Time Grant Opportunities

Because of the array of staffing options, the grant field is attractive to librarians seeking a new or additional job. Part-time positions allow for flexible schedules for those with school-age children. Freelancing from home can be combined with caregiving responsibilities, whether one is looking after the old or the young. Though some face-to-face meetings are required throughout the grant development process, much of the work—including finding the funding source, researching the need, gathering supporting data, and writing the grant—can be done from home.

Beginning Your Grant Career

The best way to break into grant writing is to write a grant. Though that sounds facile, it is serious. Nothing can substitute for the experience of preparing a proposal. Many library schools require students to study grant preparation before they graduate, and the faculty teaching this skill know that actually preparing a grant proposal is the best method for students to learn the process. In most classes, students are assigned the task of finding a grant, creating an imaginary project, and drafting a proposal and budget for submission.

The same applies for librarians interested in learning the craft. Workshops on how to write grants are available through community education programs, nonprofit organizations, and college business courses. Some offerings are free, while others cost hundreds of dollars. At some point in the instruction, almost all of these trainings will require participants to write a grant. The real learning takes place in the doing.

Team Writing

Those who would rather not undertake grant writing alone could join with others to accomplish the task. A series of grant development classes created for librarians at my college used this approach to ease librarians into grant development. After learning about grant sources and the elements of a proposal, the librarians were divided into teams. Each team was assigned a preselected grant opportunity for which a proposal and budget had to be created. Finished proposals were submitted to the preselected grant sources, but unfortunately no actual funding resulted. Subsequent workshop evaluations suggested that the process would have been improved if the teams had been allowed to identify their own grant sources. However, all of the librarians reported they had gained a better understanding of the grant process.

Volunteer Opportunities

Those intimidated by the grant development process but unable to join a grant team may want to offer to assist someone else developing a grant. Assuming a lesser responsibility, such as identifying a funding opportunity or researching data, affords the librarian an opportunity to glimpse the process from within. This limited approach also allows the volunteer to observe the various elements involved in grant development without taking on more responsibility than is comfortable.

Shadowing a grant writer is another avenue for librarians to see the various stages in proposal development. Finding a grant professional willing to be shadowed may prove difficult. To be successful, you may need to approach the potential shadowee with a more clearly defined request. "Could I see how you research the needs section?" would be better than, "Could I watch you write a grant?" If your first stab at shadowing proves successful, invitations to shadow subsequent steps in the process may follow.

One further suggestion on how to get involved would be to enter the field like I did: by serving on a screening committee for a grant professional. Some large organizations—especially those that are publicly funded—use outside individuals to help select candidates for positions. By studying the posted job requirements and meeting the candidates, the librarian may gain the confidence to pursue a grant position. After seeing the types of individuals who apply for grant jobs, the librarian may conclude: "Heck, I could do that myself." The rest—as they say—would be history.

Seeking Grant Professional Certifications

One other method for librarians to enter the grant profession is to seek one of several available professional certifications. The main advantage to obtaining certification is that it automatically establishes your credentials within the profession. Just like the letters MLS after your name, the certification program's abbreviations let people know you have successfully mastered the knowledge required by the field.

Librarians considering this route should understand that some are not convinced of the value of certification. "No one has ever asked me about my certifications," said one experienced grant consultant. "They just want to know about my success rate getting grants."

Others disagree, finding professional certification to be an effective way to announce one's ability to craft successful grant proposals. Those who want to pursue certification have several programs to choose from. The Grant Professional Certification is administered through the Grant Professionals Certification Institute (or GPCI, pronounced *gypsy*). This certification "measures an individual's ability to provide quality grant-related services within an ethical framework" and is awarded upon successfully passing an exam. Subjects covered by the exam include grant applications, project design, research knowledge, ethical standards, and post-award grant management practices.[6]

The American Grant Writers' Association offers the Certified Grant Writer credential, rewarded to those who pass a six-hour exam in grant researching, budgeting, professional ethics, and proposal writing.[7]

For those interested in the broader field of fundraising, several different certification programs are available. The CFRE (Certified Fund Raising Executive) is administered by CFRE International. This program was formed in 1997 when the Association for Healthcare Philanthropy and the Association of Fundraising Professionals merged their certification programs. The CFRE award is meant to demonstrate knowledge, skills, and commitment to ethical standards in the philanthropic sector. As of 2011, there were more than four thousand individuals who had attained the CFRE designation in the United States.[8]

A more advanced certification, the ACFRE (Advanced Certified Fundraising Executive), known as the PhD of fundraising, is administered through the Association of Fundraising Professionals. This credential indicates the holder "possesses senior level fundraising knowledge, skills, leadership, management and professional standards." To be eligible for this award, the applicant must possess the CFRE and have at least ten years of experience in the field.[9]

Several colleges and nonprofit organizations offer their own fundraising certificates, but these are usually certificates of completion rather than formally recognized certification programs.

A push for more extensive certification of grant professionals is expected in the future. National efforts are under way to establish certifications for grant writers. The Training and Certification Work Group of the federal Grants Policy Committee, under the auspices of the U.S. Chief Financial Officers Council, is charged with "developing standards for a government-wide grants management training curriculum and certification program" that would include training, competencies, certification, and the creation of a grants management database.[10] Librarians considering pursuing a career as a grant professional may want to consider adding some grant-legitimizing initials after their name if they are serious about combining librarianship with a grant development career.

NOTES

1. "Intern—Educational Foundation (Delray Beach) Research Non-Profit," Employ Florida Marketplace, accessed July 16, 2011, https://www.employflorida.com/.

2. Code of Ethics, Grant Professional Association, revised October 5, 2011, http://grantprofessionals.org/about/ethics.

3. Salary and Demographic Survey Results, Grant Professionals Association, August 30, 2010, https://grantprofessionals.org/images/docs/Surveys/Salary_Survey/2010_Salary_Survey_FINAL.pdf.

4. Entrepreneur Press and Preethi Burkholder, *Start Your Own Grant-Writing Business* (New York: Entrepreneur Press, 2008), 3–4.

5. Ibid.

6. See http://www.grantcredential.org/.

7. See http://www.agwa.us/certifiedgrantwritercredential.

8. According to http://www.cfre.org/about.html.

9. See http://www.afpnet.org/files/ContentDocuments/ACFREbrochure.pdf.

10. See http://www.cfoc.gov/index.cfm?function=GPCworkgroups.

10
CONCLUSION

The late Kathleen de la Peña McCook noted that there are "countless examples" of librarians working in partnership through grants and other sources of funding.[1] The following examples of successful projects are simply a sampling of such successes intended to inspire more such endeavors.

SUCCESS STORIES

A Library-Based Research Center

One prime example of a library successfully securing "other people's money" through grant collaboration is (Miami) Florida International University's GIS (Geographic Information Systems) Center. By providing geographic information to university departments and the public, in the last six years alone the center has led or participated in grants totaling more than $5 million, with more than $1.3 going directly to support the center.[2]

This library-based information center was the result of the happy accident that the university needed the capacity to generate geographic information but had no geography department. Being a universal service-orientated unit for all university departments, the library was chosen to establish a centralized GIS facility to service multiple academic departments in both research and teaching.

The center's charges for research begin at $75 per hour for an initial consultation, with total costs ranging from $200 to "significant amounts," according to Jennifer Fu, head of the center. Some departments repurpose grant funds to pay for the research. One linguistics professor found grant funds to pay the library $6,000 to map out the world's languages. Ten thousand dollars was the price paid for spatial analysis to support a National Science Foundation grant. Other collaborators in grant activities with the library have included the biology, urban studies, engineering, environmental science, and landscape architecture departments.

The center's teaching laboratories also host a fifteen-credit graduate certificate in GIS. "It has worked out beautifully," says Fu, especially because the library is viewed as "neutral territory" that can serve all.

Library-Based Nonprofit Centers

To help local nonprofit organizations locate and apply for grants, file taxes, and complete incorporation forms, the Vigo County Public Library in Terre Haute, Indiana, created a portal of links for community groups. Through the library's Non-Profit Information and Resources Project, more than fifteen local organizations created and hosted informational websites. According to systems and reference librarian Jeanne Holba Puacz, "What started as a simple idea for making information about local nonprofit organizations more accessible . . . developed into a profitable partnership between the library, the local nonprofits, and the community."[3]

The Williamsburg (VA) Regional Library became "a go-to resource for community leaders," thanks to the creation of a Funding Research Center. By partnering with the Williamsburg Community Health Foundation, the library provides information on grants and grant writing to local nonprofits.[4]

The Anderson County (SC) Library and United Way teamed up to create a Center for Non-Profit Excellence. Through a variety of facets—including sessions on proposal writing—the library helps nonprofits succeed.[5]

The USDA and Libraries

The Avon Grove (PA) Free Library may be a small-town library (serving a population of just over 20,000), but several years ago it earned an "exemplary community partner" designation from the USDA. In conjunction with Penn State University's Cooperative Extension Program, 4-H, and the USDA's Children, Youth, and Families at Risk (CYFAR) Program, and with the help of donated technology, the library provided instruction to young people and their families in basic computer skills.

The initial collaboration was only the beginning. According to the library's Barbara Heiderscheidt, this involvement led to further collaboration with CYFAR's Migrant Education Program, which in turn led to informal alliances resulting in bilingual story-time offerings. By reaching out to community groups, she was "able to make connections that lead to new library service."[6]

Miami Dade College and Miami-Dade County Public School's partnership with the USDA's National Agricultural Library resulted in librarians and teachers from both organizations receiving advanced training in agricultural and science research. Along with providing for onsite training, the $168,000 USDA grant enhanced the science collection at the college and high school. A paid summer internship at the National Agricultural Library inspired one college student to pursue advanced education at Stanford University.

Grant Classes at the Library

Grant-writing workshops that were fee-based became free at the Kanawha County (VA) Public Library. The program was a "huge success" and empowered the library to do more.[7]

Classes in grant proposal writing, fundraising, and marketing were just a few of the offerings available at the Greensboro (NC) Public Library, thanks to a partnership between Duke University's Nonprofit Management Certificate Program and the library's Nonprofit Resource Center.[8]

Domestic Violence Library Collaboration

One grant writer began her career in the late 1970s by seeking out the help of librarians at the Thief River Falls (MN) Public Library. According to Grant Professionals Association national board member Doris Jean Ann Heroff, GPC, "the librarians there were extremely helpful throughout the process." Not only did she receive help with the research and writing of the proposal, the library also helped manage the newly funded Domestic Violence Education Project, culminating in funding for a shelter for battered women.[9]

School and Camp Collaborations

Teachers' guides, curriculum support, class presentations, and after-school programs are just a few of the services offered by the Multnomah County (OR) Library School Corps to area K–12 educators.[10] The program also delivers "buckets of books" to summer camps, a service also offered through collaborations between other libraries' children's departments and area day camps.[11]

Award-Winning Community Collaborations

In recognition of the library's "commitment to public service through innovative programs and community partnerships," the Institute of Museums and Library Services bestowed upon the Johnson County (KS) Library its 2005 National Award for Museum and Library Service. Among the myriad of collaborations by the library, which has a strategic plan to encourage partnerships, were a "Community Issues 101" forum to encourage citizen deliberation and exchange and a Changing Lives through Literature Program, one of the nation's first alternative-sentencing literature discussion programs for teens.[12]

OPPORTUNITIES TO EXPLOIT

What all of these successes have in common is that they each resulted from seizing opportunities. The Avon Grove Library identified a need for bilingual children's services while working with the migrant community. Bilingual storytimes followed. At the Vigo County Public Library, one of the reference librarians noticed that many small nonprofit organizations did not have websites and a library-based nonprofit community portal was formed.

Each of these examples demonstrates how the first step to successful grant collaboration is seeing a need. Next, a way to fill that need is identified. Then the librarian pounces. The result: collaborative success.

SUCCESS BREEDS SUCCESS

In many cases, only one successful venture is needed because success breeds success. Just as the rich get richer, libraries that are involved in successful collaborative grants are more likely to be involved in future grants. Libraries that secure outside funding will be "perceived as a dynamic, integral part of the larger body."[13] "When library directors demonstrate that they can attract outside funding," says librarian-author Marylaine Block, "they get increased support."[14]

Former Kankakee (IL) Public Library director Cynthia Fuerst credits her recognized credibility to winning grants. "It had much to do with the subsequent willingness of the city's leadership and business community to construct a new library."[15]

COLLABORATION: A FINAL WORD

It is worth repeating the late Kathleen de la Peña McCook's comparison of the world of nonprofit collaboration to a giant jigsaw puzzle: "The pieces just need to be put in place."[16] This book has argued that libraries are ideally positioned to put many of these pieces together—and that they stand to benefit directly from doing so. Several factors would need to fall into place for libraries to assume such a role.

Risk Taking

The stereotypical librarian is not an avid risk taker. Though skydiving and cliff-climbing librarians exist, the act of putting oneself in a perilous position is not associated with the library profession. However, librarians need to do just that as a first step toward library grant collaboration.

To return to the courtship metaphor, the librarian is the one who needs to ask the person to dance. Risky, indeed, for a humiliating head shake and "no thanks" may be the response. But unless the library makes the first move, chances are slim to nil it will be approached first.

Opportunity Awareness

The library needs to be aware of opportunities in order to exploit them. The chapter on finding grant developers (chapter 3) suggests how to go about locating such opportunities. Some may be no further than your own reference desk. Others could be on the floor above you, in the building down the street, or in an office across town. Chance encounters with community members—at dinner parties, weddings, or even funerals—may yield opportunities for collaborative endeavors. It's like that old proverb, "When the student is ready, the teacher will appear": when the librarian is ready, the grant collaborative partner will appear. But this will only happen when the librarian is open to exploring possibilities and ready to take risks (see above).

Pounce on Possibilities

Once an opportunity is identified, the librarian will need to overcome any hesitancy and act. Or, to put it another way, be prepared to pounce. Make that call to the director. Go tour that building. E-mail the board president. Though it may be scary, you must take the first step to begin the partnership conversation.

Remember Research

"Remember Research" is the librarian's equivalent of "Remember the Alamo." The library's ability to locate funding sources and gather data to support needs statements is invaluable to grant seekers. Use the library's research ability to get a library representative to the grant development table. That's where the real action happens.

THE FUTURE OF LIBRARY GRANT COLLABORATION

The future of library grant collaboration is rosy. As has been discussed, several forces are pushing for more cross-institutional collaboration. The "silo era" has ended. No longer can funders afford to support single institutions, each serving its own clientele. Especially ripe for collaboration are agencies providing similar services, whether across town or across the country. Collaboration across political, geographic, or demographic borders will become mandatory requirements for many funding opportunities.

Libraries are perfectly positioned to benefit from the call for collaboration. Inherently able to serve all constituencies within their community, the library can be written into virtually any project. If nothing else, the library can always use more resources on whatever topic the project will address.

The major hurdle to incorporating the library into other organizations' grants is the difficulty of finding out about them. Several ways to surmount this obstacle have been discussed in this book. One additional suggestion would be to create a mechanism for exchanging information about the needs of community organizations. A decade ago Professor McCook called for the creation of an office within ALA for national community building. Perhaps it is now time to create such a national office for community collaboration and information sharing. Or such an office could be located at the state or regional level. Or better yet, the library could assume this role.

Information and referral were introduced as central components of library service more than thirty years ago. The time has come to transform information and referral into a community networking resource. By creating a place for organizations to share information about their future projects, the library would learn who plans to do what. By offering to conduct research to support the new program—whatever that may be— the library could insinuate itself into the development process. Hopefully, the end result will be a flow of funds into the library from other people's money.

NOTES

1. Kathleen de la Peña McCook, *A Place at the Table: Participating in Community Building* (Chicago: American Library Association, 2000), 81.

2. Jennifer Fu, e-mail message to author, September 6, 2011.

3. Jeanne Holba Puacz, "Libraries + Nonprofits Add Up to Profitable Community Partnerships," *Computers in Libraries,* 20, no. 2 (February 2005), 15.

4. Marylaine Block, *The Thriving Library: Successful Strategies for Challenging Times* (Medford, NJ: Information Today, 2007), 58.

5. See http://www.unitedwayofanderson.org/Center_for_Non_Profit_Excellence.php.

6. As quoted in McCook, 66, 67.

7. Olivia Bravo, e-mail posting to Foundation Center's Network of Cooperating Collections CCNet, "Re: Successes and Goals," December 30, 2009, http://members.boardhost.com/cctalk/msg/1262182805.html.

8. Block, 111.

9. Doris Heroff, e-mail to GPA Community Forum, General Member Forum, September 15, 2011.

10. Block, 64.

11. "Turning Community Partnerships into Dollars," Lyrasis, PowerPoint presentation, May 11, 2010.

12. McCook, 82; Marsha Bennett, "Johnson County Library Receives National Award at White House Ceremony," *Kansas Libraries* (February 2006), http://skyways.lib.ks.us/news/publish/article_00114.shtml.

13. Patricia Senn Breivik and E. Burr Gibson, "Operating within a Parent Institution," in *Funding Alternatives for Libraries,* ed. Breivik and Gibson (Chicago: American Library Association, 1979), 127.

14. Block, 105.

15. As quoted in Block, 106.

16. McCook, 3.

Knowing that I was a librarian, a grant writer for a regional hospital approached me at a local meeting of the Grant Professionals Association.

"How do I get a librarian to help me with a grant?" she asked.

"Have you asked the librarian at your hospital?" I responded, knowing the hospital where she worked maintained a substantial library. "Or you could go to the public library."

"Is that OK? I mean, can I just go to the library and tell them what I need?"

"Yes, absolutely," I said.

"Oh my gosh," she said. "I had no idea."

She had no idea. As I heard those words, memories of countless library conference sessions about how to publicize library services came back to me. Here was a grant writer who had no idea library services were available to her through the library in her building or the public library down the street. For years, librarians have tried to devise ways to promote what they have to offer. And here was a grant professional who needed the library's help but did not know how to get it. Somehow, communication between librarians and grant developers is not occurring. It reminds me of O. Henry's classic story "The Gift of the Magi," where a young married couple lacks crucial knowledge about each other.

Obviously, this book—published by the American Library Association—is directed at librarians. But the information presented here is also needed by grant professionals, nonprofit officials, and others who develop grants. Indeed, one could argue that the knowledge contained here would be of greater value to them than to library professionals. But somehow the word is not reaching that population.

And so, as an afterword to all of the librarians reading this book, I encourage you to share this information with those who develop grants. Naturally, the first step to accomplish this would be to identify those in your community who write grants. If you don't know any grant developers, see the chapter on how to find them.

Once you have identified a likely target, make sure that she gets a copy of this book. Preferably, you will buy multiple copies and send one to each grant developer you know. (If you don't know any grant developers, go ahead and buy multiple copies anyway!)

If your library budget won't allow for multiple copies, consider buying one library copy, which you could check out and send to one prospective grant developer at a time. You could even include a note that no overdue fines will be charged if they include the library as a collaborative grant partner.

AFTERWORD TO GRANT DEVELOPERS

If you are a grant developer who has received a copy of this book from a librarian, congratulations. Your project and organization are about to be enhanced through the skills and abilities the library has to offer.

But if you are a grant developer who came across this publication without library intervention, I encourage you to seek out a librarian before you launch into your next project. No matter the type of organization you represent or where you are located, a librarian is available to help you, free of charge. Public libraries are available in all parts of the country. With just a quick phone call, visit, or e-mail, you can be on your way to improving your grant proposal through library assistance. If you are in an accredited academic institution, you have access to a library right where you are. Schools have access to media centers staffed with professional media specialists. And special libraries—like the one at the hospital mentioned above—are equipped and staffed with librarians right there in the building where they work.

Each type of library listed above is represented by at least one professional organization. For a list of these organizations, see the end of this book. Any of these groups should be able to lead you to a library in your area that could cooperate with you on a grant project.

If you are interested in working with a library science student intern, you could contact a graduate school of library and information science. A searchable database of ALA-accredited programs is available at ALA.org. Working with a library science student will not afford you an opportunity to partner with a library (unless that person is also employed by a library while attending school), but you could still benefit from the student's research abilities.

Library-Enhanced Grant Services

No matter how or where you find a librarian, I can guarantee you that you will be glad you did. Your proposal will be stronger because of the librarian's involvement. The preceding pages provide details on the ways librarians can assist grant developers. Here's a summary:

> *Grant identification.* Libraries have access to online and print resources that will identify grant opportunities.
>
> *Needs statement research.* Professional librarians can provide specific data to support the need for your grant project.
>
> *Collaborative partnership.* Libraries make perfect partners, offering services and collections for every subject.
>
> *Project activities and services.* Libraries can collaborate with your project by providing workshops, classes, resource lists, and special collections.
>
> *Last-minute budget expenditures.* Library support provides a quick and effective method for using leftover funds while meeting your project objectives.
>
> *Advisory committee/evaluation assistance.* As objective, neutral, trusted organizations, libraries are valued participants for evaluative efforts.
>
> And much more . . .

Along with all of these, librarians also bring some intangible benefits. Librarians make valuable team players and usually possess the personalities and mind-set needed for effective collaboration. With a long and glorious tradition of cooperation, librarians instinctively know how to work with others to accomplish goals. And many librarians come to the profession with a degree in English or an ability to write, edit, or proofread that could be helpful for developing proposals.

Invite Librarians to Join

In the pages of this book librarians learned how to benefit from other people's money by insinuating themselves into nonlibrary grants. But subterfuge should not be necessary. Grant developers should welcome the involvement of librarians. Instead of librarians maneuvering to get to the grant table, they should be invited to join from the very beginning of the process. Actually, they should be included before it begins. Unfortunately, many grant developers do not realize how easy it is to involve librarians in grant development.

I urge grant developers to make it easier for librarians. Don't make them foist themselves on you. Instead, invite them to join you. Too often the library is not invited because grant developers never consider the library as a potential grant collaborator. But for the sake of the developing grant, the organization sponsoring the grant, and the library itself, this needs to change. The grant developer, grant-seeking organization, and library will all benefit through library grant collaboration, and with luck, more money will begin flowing for everyone to share.

SELECTED BIBLIOGRAPHY AND ADDITIONAL SOURCES

SELECTED BIBLIOGRAPHY AND WORKS CITED

American Library Association. *The Big Book of Library Grant Money*. Chicago: American Library Association, 2007.

Annual Register of Grant Support. New Providence, RI: R. R. Bowker, 1969–. Published annually.

Barbato, Joseph, and Danielle S. Furlich. *Writing for a Good Cause: The Complete Guide to Crafting Proposals and Other Persuasive Pieces for Nonprofits*. New York: Simon and Schuster, 2000.

Barber, Daniel M. *Finding Funding: The Comprehensive Guide to Grant Writing*. 2nd ed. Long Beach, CA: Bond Street Publishers, 2002.

Block, Marylaine. *The Thriving Library: Successful Strategies for Challenging Times*. Medford, NJ: Information Today, 2007.

Breivik, Patricia Senn, and E. Burr Gibson. "Operating within a Parent Institution." In *Funding Alternatives for Libraries*, edited by Breivik and Gibson, 124–128. Chicago: American Library Association, 1979.

Brown, Larissa Golden, and Martin John Brown. *Demystifying Grant Seeking*. San Francisco: Jossey-Bass, 2001.

Browning, Beverly A. *Grant Writing for Dummies*. 2nd ed. Hoboken, NJ: Wiley Publishers, 2005.

Burkholder, Preethi. *Start Your Own Grant-Writing Business*. New York: Entrepreneur Press, 2008.

Carlson, Mim. *Winning Grants Step by Step*. 2nd ed. San Francisco: Jossey-Bass, 2002.

Carter-Black, Alexis. *Getting Grants: The Complete Manual of Proposal Development and Administration*. 2nd ed. Bellingham, WA: Self-Counsel Press, 2010. Includes CD-ROM.

Clarke, Cheryl A. *Storytelling for Grantseekers: A Guide to Creative Nonprofit Fundraising*. 2nd ed. San Francisco: Jossey-Bass, 2009.

Crowther, Janet L., and Barry Trott. *Partnering with Purpose: A Guide to Strategic Partnership Development for Libraries and Other Organizations*. Westport, CT: Libraries Unlimited, 2004.

Curry, Elizabeth A. "Play with the Slinky: Learning to Lead Collaboration through a Statewide Training Project Aimed at Grants for Community Partnerships." *Resource Sharing and Information Networks* 18, nos. 1–2 (2005): 25–48.

Decker, Lance. *Over My Dead Body! A Workbook for Community Involvement*. Phoenix, AZ: Lindworth Press, 2005.

Dempsey, Beth. "Cashing In on Service: Entrepreneurial Ventures Make Money and Extend the Library's Mission." *Library Journal*, November 1, 2004.

Directory of Building and Equipment Grants. Loxahatchee, FL: Research Grant Guide, 1988–. Biennial.

Foundation Center (serial publications, dates vary)
> *Grants for Children and Youth*
> *Grants for Information Technology*
> *Grants for Libraries and Information Services*
> *Grants for Women and Girls*
> *National Guide to Funding in Arts and Culture*
> *National Guide to Funding for Libraries and Information Services*
> *National Directory of Corporate Giving*

Foundation Fundamentals. 8th ed. New York: Foundation Center, 2008.

Frey, Robert S. *Successful Proposal Strategies for Small Businesses*. 4th ed. Boston: Artech House, 2004.

Gerding, Stephanie K., and Pamela H. MacKellar. *Grants for Libraries: A How-to-Do-It Manual for Librarians*. New York: Neal-Schuman Publishers, 2006. Includes CD-ROM.

Grayson, Harriet. *Guide to Government Grants Writing: Tools for Success*. New York: iUniverse, 2005.

Harney, Ericka. "Creating Impact with Policymakers: Cases of Building Cross-Sector Partnerships to Build Stronger Programs and Grant Applications." *Journal of the American Association of Grant Professionals* (Fall 2009): 16–24.

Harris, Dianne. *Complete Guide to Winning Effective and Award-Winning Grants: Step-by-Step Instructions.* Ocala, FL: Atlantic Publishers, 2008. Includes CD-ROM.

Howlett, Susan, and Renée Bourque. *Getting Funded: The Complete Guide to Writing Grant Proposals.* 5th ed. Seattle, WA: Word and Raby Publishers, 2010.

Huxham, Chris, and Siv Vagen. *Managing to Collaborate: The Theory and Practice of Collaborative Advantage.* London: Routledge, 2005.

Improving Stakeholder Collaboration: A Special Report on the Evaluation of Community-Based Health Efforts. Group Health Community Foundation, Seattle, WA, [2001]. http://www.cche.org/pubs/ghcf-publication-stakeholder-collaboration.pdf.

Karsh, Ellen, and Arlen Sue Fox. *The Only Grant-Writing Book You'll Ever Need.* New York: Basic Books, 2009.

Koch, Deborah S. *How to Say It: Grantwriting.* New York: Prentice Hall, 2009.

Kolowich, Steve. "Embedded Librarians." *Inside Higher Ed,* June 9, 2010. http://www.insidehighered.com/news/2010/06/09/hopkins.

Landau, Herbert B. *Winning Library Grants: A Game Plan.* Chicago: American Library Association, 2011.

Levinson, Jay Conrad, Rick Frishman, and Jill Lublin. *Guerrilla Publicity: Hundreds of Sure-Fire Tactics to Get Maximum Sales for Minimum Dollars.* Avon, MA: Adams Media, 2002.

Margolin, Judith B., and Gail T. Lubin, eds. *The Foundation Center's Guide to Winning Proposals II.* New York: Foundation Center, 2005.

Mattessich, Paul W., Marta Murray-Close, and Barbara R. Monsey. *Collaboration: What Makes It Work.* 2nd ed. St. Paul, MN: Wilder Foundation, 2001.

McCook, Kathleen de la Peña. *A Place at the Table: Participating in Community Building.* Chicago: American Library Association, 2000.

McDermott, Irene E. "Get Outta Here and Get Me Some Money, Too." *Searcher* 14, no. 7 (July/August 2006): 13–17.

McGuire, Michael. "Collaborative Public Management: Assessing What We Know and How We Know It." *Public Administration Review* 66, no. s1 (December 2006): 33–43.

Michaels, Marty. "Grant-Making Overhaul at Ford Emphasizes Collaboration and Efficiency." *Chronicle of Philanthropy,* April 23, 2009. Academic Search Complete, EBSCOhost.

Milward, H. Brinton., and Keith G. Provan. *A Manager's Guide to Choosing and Using Collaborative Networks.* Washington, DC: IBM Center for the Business of Government, 2006.

Miner, Jeremy T., and Lynn E. Miner. *Proposal Planning and Writing.* 4th ed. Westport, CT: Greenwood Press, 2008.

New, Cheryl Carter, and James Aaron Quick. *How to Write a Grant Proposal.* Hoboken, NJ: John Wiley & Sons, 2003.

Norris-Tirrell, Dorothy, and Joy A. Clay. *Strategic Collaboration in Public and Nonprofit Administration.* New York: CRC Press, 2010.

Puacz, Jeanne Holba. "Libraries + Nonprofits Add Up to Profitable Community Partnerships." *Computers in Libraries* 20, no. 2 (February 2005): 13–15.

Robinson, Andy. *Grassroots Grants: An Activist's Guide to Grantseeking.* 2nd ed. San Francisco: Jossey-Bass, 2004.

Smith, Bucklin & Associates, Inc. *Complete Guide to Nonprofit Management.* 2nd ed. Edited by Robert H. Wilbur. New York: John Wiley & Sons, 2000.

Smith, Nancy Burke, and E. Gabriel Works. *Complete Book of Grant Writing: Learn to Write Grants Like a Professional.* Naperville, IL: Sourcebooks, 2006.

Stinson, Karen, and Phyl Renninger. *Collaboration in Grant Development and Management.* Washington, DC: Thompson Publishing Group, 2007.

Teitel, Martin. *"Thank You for Submitting Your Proposal": A Foundation Director Reveals What Happens Next.* Medfield, MA: Emerson and Church, 2006.

Thompson, Waddy. *The Complete Idiot's Guide to Grant Writing.* 2nd ed. Indianapolis, IN: Alpha Books, 2007. Includes CD-ROM.

Wells, Michael K. *Grantwriting Beyond the Basics.* Books 1–3. Portland, OR: Portland State University Continuing Education Press, 2005–2007.

Yang, Otto O. *Guide to Effective Grant Writing: How to Write a Successful NIH Grant Application.* New York: Kluwer Academic, 2005.

ADDITIONAL SOURCES

Blogs

CharityChannel Professional Discussion Groups, http://charitychannel.com/discussion-groups

Grants Champion Blog, http://www.grantschampion.com/blog/

Library Grants, http://www.librarygrants.blogspot.com/

PND Philanthropy New Digest, http://foundationcenter.org/pnd/

Grant Sources

ALA Awards and Grants, http://www.ala.org/ala/awardsgrants/

American Association of School Librarians, http://www.ala.org/aasl/aaslawards/aaslawards

Council of Foundation's Community Foundation Locator, http://www.cof.org/whoweserve/community/resources/index.cfm

Grants.gov, http://www.grants.gov/

Institute of Museum and Library Services, http://www.imls.gov/

National Endowment for the Arts, http://www.nea.gov/

National Endowment for the Humanities, http://www.neh.gov/grants/index.html

National Library of Medicine, http://www.nlm.nih.gov/grants.html

SLA Scholarships and Grants, http://www.sla.org/content/resources/scholargrant/index.cfm

National Assembly of State Arts Agencies, http://www.nasaa-arts.org/About/About-State-Arts-Agencies.php

State Departments of Education, http://wdcrobcolp01.ed.gov/Programs/EROD/org_list.cfm?category_ID=SEA

State Humanities Councils, http://www.neh.gov/whoweare/statecouncils.html

State Libraries and Archives, http://www.publiclibraries.com/state_library.htm

State Library Associations, http://www.ala.org/ala/mgrps/affiliates/chapters/state/stateregional.cfm

U.S. Department of Education, http://www2.ed.gov/fund/grant/apply/grantapps/index.html

Other Publications

Chronicle of Philanthropy, http://www.philanthropy.com/

Grants for Libraries Hotline, http://store.westlaw.com/grants-libraries-hotline/139015/40560036/productdetail

Humanities, http://www.neh.gov/news/humanities/2011-01/contents.html

Institute of Museum and Library Services Newsletter *Primary Source*, http://www.imls.gov/signup.aspx

RFPs and Bulletin Notices of Awards Foundation Center; send e-mail request to pndrfp@foundationcenter.org

Additional Resources

Foundation Center, http://foundationcenter.org/

Foundation Center Online Tutorials, http://www.grantspace.org/Classroom

Funding, http://www.webjunction.org/funding

Grantsmanship Center, http://www.tgci.com/

NLG Project Planning: A Tutorial, http://test.imls.gov/Project_Planning/index.asp

Foundation Finder, http://foundationcenter.org/findfunders/

Service Clubs or Civic Organizations That Provide Funding, Michigan State University, http://staff.lib.msu.edu/harris23/grants/servicec.htm

Professional Associations

American Association of School Librarians, http://www.ala.org/aasl/

American Evaluation Association, http://www.eval.org/

American Grant Writer's Association, http://www.agwa.us/

American Library Association, http://www.ala.org/

Association of College and Research Libraries, http://www.ala.org/acrl/

Association of Fundraising Professionals, http://www.afpnet.org/

Grant Professionals Association, http://grantprofessionals.org/

Public Library Association, http://www.ala.org/pla/

Reference and User Services Association, http://www.ala.org/rusa/

Special Libraries Association, http://www.sla.org/

INDEX

A

activities, grant component, 10–11
administrative costs, 48
administrator, grant team member role, 30
Advanced Certified Fundraising Executive (ACFRE), 67
advisory committees, 22, 76
Alliance of Information and Referral Systems (AIRS), 22
American Evaluation Association, 21
American Grant Writer's Association (AGWA), 20, 67
American Library Association (ALA), 57
announcements for grants, 11
applications, collaboration and, 60
approval, importance of, 61
articles, publicizing and, 51
assessment of program, 50
Association of American Grant Professionals, 19
Association of Fundraising Professionals (AFP), 20, 67
Association of Healthcare Philanthropy, 67
associations, as partner, 57
audits, internal and external, 60
award winners, 20, 71
awards, grant sizes and, 8

B

bilingual storytime (success story), 71
biographical paragraphs or resumes, 12
Block, Marylaine, 24, 35, 72
boards, as grant resource, 22–23
book vendors and distributors, 52
Breivik, Patricia Senn, 2, 61

Buckets of Books (success story), 71
budgets
    development of, 45
    expenditures and, 52, 76
    finance experts, team member role, 30
    grant component, 11
    narrative for, 45–46
    spending allocations, 51–52

C

camp collaborations, 71
career development, grants and, 40
careers, grant-writing types, 63–67
Catalog of Federal Domestic Assistance (database), 37
Center for Non-Profit Excellence (success story), 70
certifications, grant professional, 67
Certified Fund Raising Executive (CFRE), 67
Certified Grant Writer (credential), 67
Changing Lives through Literature Program (success story), 71
children's activities, grants and, 48
citizen boards, 23
civic associations, as grant resources, 33
classes, grant-writing, 70–71
Clay, Joy A., 30
coalitions, subject-specific, 22
Coffman, Steve, 2
collaborating
    activities and, 10
    applications and, 60
    approaching potential partners, 57–58
    continued success of, 71–73

creating partnerships, 35
finding developers, 17–27
libraries and, 56–57
MOU and, 59
needs-based, 23–24
partnerships, 7–8, 53, 76
precautions, 60–61
reasons for, 55–56
school and camp, 71
committees
    advisory, 22, 76
    grants policy, 67
    internal review, 50
communities of opportunity office, 56
community development corps, as partners, 57
community initiatives, as partners, 57
Community Issues 101 (forum), 71
conferences, publicizing and, 51
confidentiality and grants, 41
contact logs, 19
content expert, team member role, 30
contract organizations, 19
contributions, in-kind, 49–53
Cooke, Eileen, 32
Cooperating Collections, 17
core collection online resources, 18
corporate grants, 7, 8
Corporate Philanthropy Report, 38
costs, indirect, 48
cross-institutional partnerships, mandating, 50
Crowther, Janet L., 35, 56

D

data
    collection of, 9
    examples of, 40
    as need support, 11, 39
databases, grant types, 37–38

department and individual
    involvement, 9
design teams, 29
developers
    in libraries, 17–19
    locating services, 19–22
    organizations of, 19
development steps (grant phase),
    9
direct-mail campaign, publicizing,
    51
direct support, 45–48
directories and listings, 38
Disney Institute, 56
Domestic Violence Education
    Project (success story), 71

E

economic development, grants
    and, 40
editing and writing assistance,
    25
editors, team member role, 30
Education Grants Alert, 38
elderly services, 23
empowerment zones, as grant
    resource, 22
Encyclopedia of Associations, 21
ethical funding agency personnel,
    21
evaluations
    assistance for, 76
    grant component, 12–13
    of organizations, 19
    programs for, 50
evaluators, 21
event sponsorship, 51
expenditures, 5, 52, 76

F

federal economic development
    grant criteria, 39
federal education grant criteria,
    12, 39
*Federal Grants and Contracts
    Weekly*, 38
federal library grant activity
    criteria, 10
Federal Register (database), 37
fee-based resources, 36
financial commitments, MOU
    and, 59
financial support, 48–49
Florida International University
    (Miami), 69
Ford Foundation, 56

formal approval, importance of, 61
formats, MOU and, 59
*Foundation and Corporate Grants
    Alert*, 38
Foundation Center Cooperating
    Collections, 8, 10, 17–18
Foundation Directory Online
    (database), 18, 37
Foundation Grants to Individuals
    (database), 7, 18, 37
Free Library of Philadelphia
    (Pennsylvania), 2
Fu, Jennifer, 69
Fuerst, Cynthia, 72
full-time opportunities, grant
    careers, 65–66
funding
    asking for, 44–45
    bringing in, 2–5
    receiving (post-award), 10
    spending allotted, 51–52
    unused, 5
Funding Alternatives for Libraries
    (ALA), 2
Funding Research Center, 70
future of grant collaboration,
    71–73

G

geographic coalitions, 22
Gibson, E. Burr, 2, 61
GIS (geographic information
    system), 41, 69
goals, collaboration and, 61
governing agencies, as grant
    resource, 22
government grants, 7
grant administrator, team member
    role, 30
grant developers
    aiding identification, 76
    aiding librarians, 3–4
    individuals as, 33
    partnering with, 4–5
    as professionals, 13
    working with, 29–34
grant development
    groups and, 25
    locating sources, 37
    process of, 7–14
    proposals, 3–4, 10–13
    requirements for, 7–9
Grant Professional Association
    (GPA), 19–20, 65
Grant Professional Certification
    Institute (GPCI), 67

grant success examples, 69–72
grant writing
    career requirements, 63–64
    careers, 63–67
    defined, 9
    future of, 73
    workshops (success story),
        70–71
granting agency, returning funds
    to, 5
GrantNavigator (database), 37
grantors, approaching, 24–26
grants
    components of, 10–13
    confidence developing, 3–4
    departments for, 23
    evaluators, 21
    library-enhanced services, 76
    time constraints, 33–34
    types and sizes, 7–8
Grants Policy Committee, 67
GrantsAlert (database), 37–38
Grants.gov (database), 37
GrantStation (database), 37
Gross, Valerie J., 56, 61
groups
    dynamics of, 30–31
    identifying, 26
GuideStar (database), 38

H

Health Grants & Contracts Weekly,
    38
Heiderscheidt, Barbara, 70
Heroff, Doris Jean Ann, 71
Holt, Glen E., 56
Huntington Public Library (New
    York), 25

I

in-kind contributions, 49
income expectations, 65
indirect costs
    defined, 48
    entitlement to, 60
indirect support, defined, 48
individual or private grants, 7
information gathering system,
    19
Institute of Museums and Library
    Services, 71
internal review committees, 50

J

journal articles, publicizing and,
    51

L

Landau, Herbert B., 7
leader, team member role, 30
lectures, grants and, 48
legislative hearing testifiers, as grant resource, 22
legislators, as grant resource, 22–23
Levinson, Jay Conrad, 35
library-based research, 36
library collaboration, activities and, 10
library-enhanced grant services, 76
Library/Learning Centers (Foundation Center), 17
library support types, 49–53
Library System and Services (LSSI), 2–3
listings and directories, 38
Long, Sarah Ann, 56

M

managing organizations, 19
Margolin, Judith B., 10
material support, 46–50
McCook, Kathleen de la Peña, 2, 69, 72
median grant awards, 8
meetings, scheduling, 58
member considerations, 31–32
memorandum of understanding (MOU), 59
Migrant Education Program (success story), 70
mission, partnerships and, 61
mission creep, 8–9
monetary support, 45–46
monitoring formats, MOU and, 59

N

narrative, grant component, 11
National Agricultural Library (Miami), 70
National Award for Museum and Library Service, 71
National Science Foundation, 8, 11–13, 69
needs-based collaborations, 23–24
needs identification, 9
needs statement
    grant component, 11–12
    locating research, 38–39
    research for, 76
neighborhood councils, as grant resource, 22

news releases, publicizing and, 51
Nielsen, Therese Purcell, 25
Non-Profit Information and Resources Project (success story), 70
nongovernmental organizations (NGOs), 21
nonprofit centers, library-based, 70
Nonprofit Management Certificate Program (Duke University), 70–71
nonprofit organizations, 21–23
nonprofit publishers, 38
Nonprofit Resource Center (NC), 70–71
Norris-Tirrell, Dorothy, 30

O

office equipment, budgets for, 47–48
officers, grant program, 20–21
officials
    local, town, and county, 23
    newly appointed, 58
online resources, 18, 36
opportunities, awareness of, 72
organizations
    joining, 19–20
    locating, 21–23
    service alignment, 9
outcomes and evaluation, grant component, 12–13
overhead, cost and, 48

P

panel presentations, grants and, 48
parameters, establishing, 43–44
parent-teacher associations, 23
part-time opportunities, 65–66
participants, responsibility and obligation, MOU and, 59
partners
    agencies, team member role, 30
    approaching, 57–59
    cautions regarding, 60–61
    collaborative, 4–5
    projects needing, 23–24
    purchasing, 55
    researching, 9
personnel
    defined, 12
    ethical funding agency, 21
    grant component, 12

phases, development of grant, 8–10
philanthropic liaison, office of, 56
A Place at the Table (McCook), 2
post-award (grant phase), 9–10, 14
pre-award (grant phase), 8–9, 14
precautions when collaborating, 60–61
preparation for request, 43–44
primary fiscal agent, defined, 60
private or individual grants, 7
programs
    evaluations of, 50
    hosting, 51
    provisions for, 48
    publicizing, 50–51
projects
    activities and services, 76
    directors for, 12
    housing considerations, 51
    partners and, 23
    post-award considerations, 10
    team considerations, 29
proofreaders
    librarians as, 25
    team member role as, 30
proposals
    development phase, 9, 14
    locating previous, 38
Puacz, Jeanne Holba, 70
public policy use, collaboration and, 24
publicity, grant component, 12
publicizing grant (post-award), 10
publicizing programs, 50–51
publishers, nonprofit, 38

Q

quality of personnel, 12

R

record-keeping, importance of, 60
recorder, team member role, 30
reference desks, as resources, 18–19
referral clearinghouses, 21–22
relationships, strengthening, 3
Renninger, Phyl, 29, 41, 55
renovations, grants and, 46–47
request for proposal (RFP), 9–13, 43–44
requirements, grant consideration, 9
research
    grants and, 4, 25
    librarians and, 35–41

research (cont.)
  library-based center, 69
  locating grant sources, 36
  skills and abilities, 35–36
  supporting needs statement,
    38–39
research center, library-based
    (success story), 69
researcher, versus subject expert,
    40–41
resources, grant developer, 17–18
responsibilities, defining, 61
resumes or biographical
    paragraphs, 12
reviews
  committees for, 50
  process of, 13
  team member role, 21
risk taking, importance of, 72
round tables, nonprofit, 23

S
salary expectations, 65
school collaborations, 71
service recipients, team member
    role, 30
services, collaborative, 35
Seward, Stephen, 3
skills, career, 63–64
sources, locating, 9
spending considerations, 10,
    51–52
staff support, 47, 48

standards, government-wide
    grants and, 67
state library grant, publicity
    example, 12–13
state workforce development
    grant criteria, 39
STEM (science, technology,
    engineering, and
    mathematics), 24, 39
Stinson, Karen, 29, 41, 55
strategic partners, identifying, 9
strategic planning, 9
structure, MOU and, 59
subject expert, versus library
    researcher, 40–41
summary, grant component, 13
support types, 45–48
sustainability, grant component,
    13
surveys, conducting, 58–59

T
team members, roles and
    characteristics, 30–31, 44
team writing careers, 66
teams, grant development types,
    29–30
technology assistant, team
    member role, 30
The Thriving Library (Block), 24
time considerations, 33–34, 59
timekeeper, team member role, 30
Tocqueville, Alexis de, 19

Training and Certification Work
    Group, 67
travel budgets, 47–48
Trott, Barry, 35, 56
tutoring, grants and, 40

U
United Way, 21, 23
U.S. Chief Financial Officers
    Council, 67
U.S. Department of Education, 8
U.S. Homeland Security grant,
    budget example, 11
USA Government Grants
    (database), 38
USDA, libraries and, 70

V
vendors, as grant resource, 23
Vigo County Public Library (IN),
    70
volunteer opportunities, 66

W
Williamsburg (VA) Community
    Health Foundation, 70
*Winning Library Grants: A Game
    Plan* (Landau), 7
writers, team member role, 30
writing and editing assistance,
    25
Writing for a Good Cause, 36
writing organizations, 19